THE SPIRITUAL
EXERCISE BOOK

THE SPIRITUAL EXERCISE BOOK

UNA KROLL

FIRETHORN PRESS

First published in Great Britain in 1985 by
Waterstone & Co. Limited
49 Hay's Mews
London W1X 7RT

Firethorn Press is an imprint of
Waterstone & Co. Limited

© 1985 Una Kroll

ISBN 0 947752 18 8 Hardback
ISBN 0 947752 65 X Paperback

Cover designed by Carol Brickley – Boldface Typesetters
Cover photograph by Andy Lane

Studio photography by Andy Lane. The publishers are also
grateful to the Tony Stone Photolibrary – London for their
kind permission to reproduce material from their collection.

Designed and Typeset by Boldface Typesetters, London EC1

Printed and bound by Richard Clay plc
The Chaucer Press
Bungay Suffolk

Distributed by Sidgwick & Jackson Limited
1 Tavistock Chambers
Bloomsbury Way
London WC1A 2SG

For Floss, Leo, Liz and Una-Maria
whose lives have enriched our
family and given us great happiness.

Acknowledgement

To Mark Booth for a splendid idea, inviting me to share it, and for his help and encouragement in making this book possible.

To Leo, my husband, for reading draft texts, making suggestions and enduring my pre-occupation with the 'work outs' over several months.

To Floss, our eldest daughter, for invaluable professional advice about the physical exercises.

To Leo, Liz and Una-Maria for a good humoured approach to the whole thing, especially when their sleep was interrupted by music and tapping typewriter.

To Betty Houghton, who carried out every single exercise and whose helpful comments have enriched the text.

To Messrs Hodder and Stoughton, publishers, by whose kind permission I have been able to include all the passages quoted from the New International version of the Holy Bible.

CONTENTS

INTRODUCTION

In my own life Christian discipleship has been a spiritual adventure which has helped me to think of each day as a new opportunity to get to know God a little better. On this adventure I've found that I've needed to spend time and energy overcoming the temptation to give in to the kind of laziness, boredom and apathy that can threaten my health, stunt my growth and reduce me to a state where I resemble a flabby pallid travesty of a Christian disciple. Other Christian friends have discovered the same need to try to keep themselves fit for God's service. Our conversations have led me to design this course of spiritual exercises for busy people, men and women of all ages, who are prepared to spend a minimum of fifteen minutes a day in enjoyable self-discipline, reflection and spiritual renewal.

This is a 'do it yourself' book written by a Christian for other Christians, but it can also be used by people searching for God who have not found themselves at home in institutional Christianity. It has been designed so that it can be used by people of different dispositions and degrees of experience who want to explore ways of renewal which can help them to grow closer to God as revealed in the person of Christ.

Experience has taught me that I can only sustain a real drive towards spiritual fitness for about two months at a time. That is why I have designed this course of spiritual exercises to last just eight weeks.

Each day's exercises are based on the Bible. The Bible is the only book that will be quoted although I have drawn on the wisdom of some great Christian writers and teachers when I have been designing the practical parts of each day's work. One of the wonderful things about the Bible is that its message is eternal; yet we hear it afresh each time we read it, and we hear it according to our individual needs at the time. We hear its message differently at different times and stages of our lives, partly also because the Bible is always showing us new areas of ourselves. So I have tried to design this course in such a way as to enable you, through the Bible, to discover strengths, talents and appetites in yourself that you haven't used before. Each day's exercises are meant to be fundamentally serious as well as fun: they can be adapted to suit your own needs once you have discovered their meaning and place in your own life.

WAKING UP TO A BETTER WAY OF LIFE

What it's like to be spiritually flabby

Each day that we live we have the chance of waking up to a new and better way of life. That's equally true when yesterday seemed like the best day of our lives to date as when we realise that our journey today and for the foreseeable future is likely to be tougher and more demanding than anything we have yet experienced.

I woke up to a new and better way of life long ago when I became a Christian, but that event did not turn out to be a passport to a smooth ride. After some two or three years as a Christian enthusiast I plummeted into a kind of hell from which I was only to be delivered some two years later by the mercy and grace of God. That kind of thing happens to young people, and I was young at the time. Nothing quite like it has happened since then, but there have been several fairly long periods when I have found myself disillusioned with the institutional church to which I belong. On other occasions I have been disillusioned with myself and so inclined to slackness. Very occasionally I have even been disinclined to believe in a God who seemed so remote and unapproachably holy.

To those beset by pain, difficulties, and distresses it may seem absurd to talk about a new and better way of life. Indeed, it would be absurd to say such a thing if I were talking about such awakenings during the times of my sufferings, but I am not. I am writing with hindsight, with gratitude for the way that God has carried many other people, including myself, through those terrible times when we have woken up to each new day with dread, when prayer has been meaningless, bible reading sterile, Christian company uncongenial and Christian witness well nigh impossible. When that kind of spiritual sickness overcomes us we cannot pretend to enjoy each day. Even if we have been forewarned to expect such difficulties in our spiritual experience, even if we know that we are being tried in the furnace of God's love through that apparent absence and silence, we usually feel bewildered, we know self-recrimination, doubt and despair that can last for weeks, months or even years, periods that seem to isolate us from other Christians. Suffering like that teaches us only if we come through it, which we can't do in our own strength, but only through the mercy and loving help of God. It is only by faith that we can overcome hardships and miseries and thank God for each day, 'at all times and in all places'.

Of course, there are many days when life has been very different for me, days when I am riding high, buoyant with joy, certain that all is well and shall be well, now and for evermore. Most of us do react to the ups and downs of life in that kind of way if we are reasonably happy. And looking back on the events of my own life, I have been aware of an undercurrent of excitement at the start of each day, largely because I can never be certain about what is going to happen at any particular moment. I know the general outline of each day, of course, and life can get rather monotonous if much the same happens day after day, but the hope is nearly always there that something interesting may be going to come along. Even when everything is rather dark and gloomy I tend to go on with the search for a new and better way of life.

It has been my belief that a new and better way of life is offered to me and to everyone who accepts Christ as Lord and this has kept me going year after year. I have thanked God time and again for the blessings of Christianity. In times of deep doubt, when I've only been able to name faith as a stubborn refusal to give up, I've tried to go on saying 'thank you', even when I haven't understood exactly what faith means. The loving support of family and friends has helped me along. Various Christian communities have provided me with lots of food for thought and made me aware that search and discovery go hand in hand. So whenever I've discovered some aspect of truth about God or experienced a new dimension of discipleship I've been able to realise that this isn't journey's end but a resting place along the way.

The Oneness of Body, Mind and Spirit

Many people have grown up with the idea that a human being is made up of three integrated parts, body, mind/soul, spirit. There is a bit of confusion as to whether the mind belongs to the body as a function of the brain, or whether it belongs to the soul as part of the 'self', that which makes each person unique and precious in God's eyes. In practice the mind bridges body and soul and feels as if it is part of both. The spirit is generally thought of as that which links us to God. It is that element in us which enables the the Holy Spirit to indwell us during our life-times and enables us to be clothed with our resurrection body after death.

This idea of our being three entities making up one person is quite useful since it allows us to think of ourselves as being able to be well in soul and spirit while our bodies are afflicted with some disease which may involve our having a broken leg, an amputated arm or a removed internal organ. It also enables us to see that a sick mind or a mental handicap does not necessarily prevent anyone from having a pure and innocent spirit held safely in God's love for all eternity.

There are, however, considerable dangers to this way of looking at human nature. Christians, individually and collectively, have fallen into the traps of this way of thinking whenever they have separated body from soul and soul from spirit, and have dealt only with one element in a person rather than with the whole. For, as we all know, though we sometimes prefer not to, a sick body can affect a person's soul and spirit: a sick spirit can certainly affect anyone's bodily health.

Medical research, of course, has effectively demonstrated the link between mind and body in relation to psychosomatic diseases such as peptic ulcers, asthma, certain kinds of high blood pressure and some forms of cancer. It has also demonstrated the existence of links between the emotional shocks which come from unemployment and bereavement and bodily illness. Scientists have been less certain about the casual relationship between spiritual sickness and bodily illness, but this link is becoming more widely accepted as our understanding of the reality of the transcendent and inexplicable experiences of people's lives is increasingly discussed and examined scientifically.

Within the last three decades or so, there has been a shift among scientists and Christians away from the idea that matter and spirit are separate entities. The dualistic attitudes that derived from this idea implied that spiritual health had nothing to do with bodily health, that spirit and matter were opposed to each other, spirit being seen as 'good' and matter as 'bad', that unpleasant spiritual activities were somehow more laudable than pleasurable bodily experiences. Many Christians were infected with dualism and came to believe that spirit and flesh were necessarily at war with each other. Moreover, many went further, linking maleness with spirit and God, and femaleness with flesh, earth and satan, and this approach had some fairly disastrous consequences in all Christian churches for the relations between men and women and for everyone's attitude towards God-given sexuality. Happily, attitudes towards the body have altered and in the place of the old attitudes have come new and recovered insights into the essential unity between matter and spirit, heaven and earth, men and women, celibacy and sexual activity in partnership. This does not mean that Satan and sin are ignored, that women and men are interchangeable or that sexual licence is encouraged, but it does mean that the body has begun to find its proper place in the Christian religion, a place it always had, since God took human flesh when Jesus Christ was born, but which had been overlaid by dualistic error.

The 'new' insights into the essential unity between matter and spirit have come largely from the physicists. The 'recovered' insights have come from the theologians. The body has recovered its importance in Christian spirituality. Body and soul have been brought together. Bodily discipline can now be seen as a good spiritual tool. Women, and all that they can bring to the life of the Church, have been increasingly welcome in many Christian communities during these last three decades. Celibacy and sexually active partnerships can be seen as creative vocations on a par with each other. Bodily involvement in worship and prayer is finding acceptance through the use of disciplined exercise, dance and drama as important aids to worship. We live in creative times.

In the past decade I, and many other people, have been able to enjoy Christian workshops, 'do it yourself' seminars and retreats where all these 'whole person', or 'holistic', insights have been put into action. I had already begun to discover the essential goodness of my own body and my womanhood some time before, but having many of my own ideas confirmed by other Christians has made a considerable difference to my own spirituality. I can now enjoy my body and its various 'pep up' activities. I can use my body in prayer and worship. I can ask God to use it, under the guidance of the Holy Spirit, to serve other people and I do, through touch and the ministry of the laying on of hands for God to use in healing people through the healing ministry of the Church. This 'whole person' approach to medicine and religion has changed the way I work as a minister of the Church who is also a practising doctor of medicine, and, I believe, has helped me to serve God in new and better ways.

The 'whole person' approach has been used in this book. The idea that body and mind and spirit must work as a team has encouraged me to link physical exercises with prayer and meditation. As you will see, neither the physical exercises in the 'Act of Commitment' part of each day's work, nor the objects used for most of the meditations, are 'special' or 'religious'. The physical exercises are of the ordinary 'keep fit' variety, enjoyed by hundreds of thousands of people who want to keep their bodies healthy. The objects are everyday household objects for the most part. It is this team work between body, mind and spirit, this marrying of our ordinary lives with our spiritual experience that seems to me to be important for many modern Christians who live busy lives, yet want to take their faith seriously, moment by moment, day by day, year after year.

This book is a Christian challenge to the fashionable work-out books that separate the soul and the spirit from the body, and then deal only with the latter. I believe they are fundamentally misguided because to me, physical fitness can only be achieved within the context of the spiritual and mental fitness of the whole person to serve God. More importantly, I think the physical fitness craze is misguided even sometimes sinful because it encourages people to rely on their own efforts rather than on the love of God and to work towards their own, narcissistic self-satisfaction rather than towards finding and fulfilling their own God-given role. As St. Paul writes:

'Do you not know that in a race all the runners run, but only one gets the prize? Run in such a way as to get the prize. Everyone who competes in the games goes into strict training. They do it to get a crown that will not last; but we do it to get a crown that will last forever. Therefore I do not run like a man running aimlessly. I do not fight like a man beating the air. No. I beat my body and make it my slave so that after I have preached to others, I myself will not be disqualified for the prize.'   (1 Cor 9:24-27)

These are the general ideas behind this book. Now we can turn to the detail of each section of the course.

HOW EACH DAY'S EXERCISES BRING YOU CLOSER TO GOD

Each day's 'session' has been timed to last fifteen minutes.

Although it can be done at any time of the day, you'll probably find it's worth dragging yourself out of bed just that bit earlier in order to get a good start to the day. Then you can literally wake up to a better way. Most of you will probably want to do each day's exercises on your own. Some may be able to join up with a spouse or other members of the family, or with friends. If this is a practical possibility it is worth considering as the enthusiasm, help and encouragement of other people can help everyone to go on until the end of the course in an easy and companionable way.

The pattern for each day is much the same. This framework isn't meant to imprison you but to provide you with a kind of 'launch pad' to the freedom of a happily disciplined Christian life.

The Act of Self-Commitment

Since the earliest days posture and controlled movement have been used by Christians. Some postures, such as kneeling, and some movements, such as raising hands into a pleading position, are known to everybody, but there are many others, and I shall be using them a lot. Where appropriate, there will be photographs to show you how to do them. Their function is to bring the body into tune with mind and spirit so that the whole being can be brought into tune with God's plan for the universe. We begin our day's spiritual exercises by making our whole being a tool for God. The concentration needed for bodily stillness or bodily movement generates a spiritual alertness to what God wants us to do. By using your body in this way you are literally making an act of self-commitment, and when you are doing the more strenuous of these acts, you should think of yourself as being like St. Paul, beating your body to make it your slave, so that you will not be disqualified from the prize.

The first stage of each day's program is meant to last for 4 minutes. When you begin the course you will probably have to time yourself with a clock. Later on, I hope you will find that your body swings into a natural rhythm and you can stop wondering whether you are taking too long or stopping too early, and concentrate all the better on the theme that I have given you for that day.

Centering down

Centering down is a way of preparing for prayer. It's a way of letting go, letting go of tension, of preoccupation with personal problems and worrisome thoughts, of all the things that can get between you and God. It's also a way of getting still and empty before God, ready to become aware of the whispers of the Holy Spirit who, 'intercedes for us with groans that words cannot express'. (Rom 8:28)

Christians down the ages have used a variety of ways of arriving at this still emptiness, and I have used several of them in the course, some of which need explanation.

Using your breathing as a way of centering your mind
Breathing is a natural rhythm which sustains our lives. When we pay attention to it with our minds we slip into a rhythm which brings our minds into harmony with our bodies.

You may find it very easy to close your eyes, slow your breathing and empty your mind of all images so that it is ready to meet God in deep silence and stillness. Many people, however, cannot do this at will or whenever they want to. If you find it difficult to empty your mind of thoughts, then I suggest that you focus your attention on your breathing, then add a simple rhythmic phrase which you can whisper to yourself, under your breath, to help yourself towards stillness. This phrase is not so much a prayer in itself as a prayerful thought which can carry you to a point beyond thought where there can be a true meeting with God.

Using the Jesus prayer as a way of centering yourself
The Jesus prayer is used a great deal by Eastern Orthodox Christians. The recurrent recitation, aloud, or quietly to oneself, of this prayer produces a kind of background music which can set the spirit free to rest in God.

The full Jesus prayer is, 'Lord Jesus Christ, son of the living God, have mercy on me, a sinner.' If you say this prayer quietly to yourself several times you'll find that its rhythm naturally falls into time with steady slow breathing. This is a prayer of adoration and penitence. It predisposes its user to humility.

Many people who have used this prayer in its full form come to prefer the shorter form which consists only of repeating the name of Jesus again and again. The simple spoken rhythm brings the mind to its natural rest in Christ.

Using visual images as a way of centering
Sometimes it is good to center down with your eyes open to beauty, feasting them on images which take you towards a meeting. Candles, water, pictures all provide images of beauty which can help you to move from vigorous activity towards intense concentration on God.

At other times it is good to close your eyes and focus them on the warm darkness which enfolds you, seeing the blackness as a friendly entrance into light, just as death is a gateway to heaven.

Using music as a help towards reaching the center
The song of a bird, the sound of a bell, the swell of the sea, the noise of rain falling on a roof, these tiny whispers of music can all take us to God. So, too, can music which has been composed by human beings. Although a few people are born tone deaf, most of us are blessed by being able to enjoy music.

Music chosen for centering down usually needs to be rhythmic and meditative. You may like to amass a small collection of music that you can use from time to time, either as a background to your centering down exercise, or as a substitute for the suggestions given for that part of a particular day's 'work out'.

Using your body and its memories to lead you to a meeting
Sometimes a memory can lead to a deep longing for a renewal of faith or a recaptured experience. There are times when it's good to use a bodily posture, such as kneeling with your hands uplifted into a pleading position, to remind you of who it is you are preparing to meet. Body language of all kinds can be important when you are preparing to pray. I have suggested using your body, its memories and associations, in several different ways during the centering down section of each day's work.

Centering down should take you about two to three minutes. With a little practice you'll soon acquire the knack. It's good to try all the different methods that are used during the next two months. You'll probably find some more attractive than others and might want to go on using them after the course is over. It may be interesting to see if the methods you find most helpful during the first couple of weeks are the same as those you enjoy at the end of our time together.

Prayer for a meeting

Once you are centered down you are ready for prayer. There are many different kinds of prayer and praise and I hope you'll go on using all the ways you are familiar with outside the course. This moment of prayer, however, is for a meeting.

It is both a joy and 'a dreadful thing to fall into the hands of the living God'. (Heb 10:31) We meet God only because of the atoning work of Christ who has enabled us to be adopted as the sons and daughters of God. Through Christ, God meets us where we are and meets us at each moment of each day of our lives. We become aware of the Holy Spirit's presence in our lives whenever we listen to or turn towards God. Our prayer for a meeting is just one way of telling God of our desire and willingness to follow Christ. It is through Christ that we pray.

In this program, I have paid particular attention to using our bodies in our prayers. I have also used very simple, well known, easy to remember phrases from psalms and Bible prayers on occasion. I would also encourage you to use your own words and wordless desires during this very brief act of self-dedication and personal commitment to discipleship.

At first you may find it good to reach out towards God, to move towards your meeting, as it were. Later on you may prefer to open your heart and wait for God to move towards you. Both ways can be right.

Meditation

Meditation is one of those words that have been a source of muddle and confusion for many modern Christians. The confusion arises because the word is used by members of other religions to describe certain specialised spiritual disciplines and mental activities such as Zen meditation and transcendental meditation. These kinds of meditation are rather different from Christian meditation, although the techniques employed in some forms of non-Christian meditation have affinities with some of the techniques used in deep relaxation or centering down exercises which some Christians use before they pray, or simultaneously with prayer.

Christian meditation is a process of prayerful looking, listening and learning over a period of time and this is the kind of meditation you will find used in this book. Christians have always thought it good to consider the events of Christ's life and the great doctrines of the Christian faith in a prayerful way. This is the approach that most great spiritual teachers like St. Francis de Sales and Ignatius Loyola have adopted and that so many of us have found helpful and adapted to our own use.

In the daily meditations which form part of this course you'll be invited to reflect on a short passage from the Bible. You've only got about seven to eight minutes each day for this part of your 'work out' but the value of each meditation does not depend upon its length so much as upon the use you can make of each minute.

Like the centering down and prayer sections, you'll find there are several different approaches used in the meditations. Nearly all of them include a bodily component in order to emphasise the goodness of using the whole of ourselves in our explorations into the mystery that is God.

You are invited to read the scripture passages aloud. Unless you've already decided to share each day's work with other people, you may feel slightly absurd doing this at first. The idea behind the invitation is to slow yourself down enough to absorb the words properly. Most of us find it easy, especially if we're in a hurry, to skim the words unless we read slowly, so reading aloud is a way of preventing ourselves from skimping this part of the meditation. If you really don't like the sound of your own voice though, please ignore the suggestion.

Each meditation ends in a concrete action. The idea behind this is to keep a firm hold on reality. It also emphasises the experiential truth that our Christian commitment necessarily leads us into action even though such action may be an interior and hidden one.

You can do all the meditations on their own so if you've got up late and simply don't have the time to fit them in along with your physical exercises and prayer time, don't worry so long as you can fit them in later. You'll probably find, though, that you'll enjoy your day's exercises best and get the most out of them if you can manage to have your fifteen minutes all in one go.

Again, timing each meditation can be a problem. Keep an eye on the clock. If you don't like doing that, and I don't, you can use quiet pre-timed taped music as a background to your meditation, or some kind of pleasant alarm like a kitchen timer or a stop watch calculator with an audible signal. Most of us will find our own rhythm within a few days. Getting long winded about our meditations is less productive in the long run than we might realise. Rushing our thoughts brings them to the surface alright but they never stick around, and seldom prove helpful to our growth, since our first thoughts about any subject may not be the ones we want to hold on to in the end. Depending on your temperament and previous experience you'll probably find a seven to eight minute meditation too short or too long at first. Well, training yourself to use the time you've got, no more, no less, will help you in all sorts of other ways as you'll discover if you try it, but please don't feel you need to be punctilious about it. I'm sure you don't time how long it takes you to get dressed each day or to eat a meal yet your average time spent on these activities will probably hardly vary from one day to the next because you've developed a natural rhythm which suits your own way of life. So it is with prayer. God helps us to find a natural rhythm in and through using our time in a disciplined way on occasions. So, don't allow yourself to become obsessed by this matter of timing, so long as you don't over run your time too often and find yourself late for work or whatever it is you have to do next.

Your fifteen minutes will have been used up by the time you have finished your meditation. This may be all that you want to and need to do each day. There are, however, two other steps you can take towards real fitness, and if you can and want to find time for them you may find one or both worthwhile.

One step is to say the same prayer at noon each day for two months. You need to choose one that you know very well, like the Lord's Prayer, so that you can say it to yourself wherever you are at that time. When I first tried this kind of disciplined use of time to bring my thoughts Godwards at regular intervals I found it remarkably difficult. Now it is easier but I still forget sometimes. God doesn't. The other step is to find time at the end of each day to reflect on what you've experienced and learnt from your day's exercises. In order to provide for those people who would find this helpful, I've included an optional extra session for each day.

Later reflection

You can spend as little as five minutes each day for this optional extra or as much as fifteen minutes. You should rarely need to spend more than this amount of time looking back. Its purpose is not 'navel gazing' but becoming more fit to serve God according to your own vocation.

With a little practice you'll find you can flop into an easy chair or on to your bed and relax quite quickly. Then you can 'center down' and cast your mind back to the earlier session. If you carry out each evening's suggestions you'll probably find yourself taking just one more step further along on your journey.

Right at the end of each section on reflection you'll find reference to keeping a spiritual journal. Christians since St. Augustine's time (4th century A.D.) have found this a helpful activity. Its use as a valuable spiritual discipline has increased within the past fifteen years.

Keeping a spiritual journal is not like keeping a diary of the events in your life, nor is it meant to be an exercise in beautiful writing suitable for literary publication at a later date. It is a private record of your reflections on and your responses to each day's journey. To it you may like to add other reflections, poems, prayers and quotations which you've found specially helpful and relevant. A spiritual journal offers you a way of noting ideas and insights you have found particularly useful at one stage of your journey. At a later date you can look back and understand where you have come from. You can also see whether you have rooted those ideas and allowed them to flower and bear fruit in your life, or, alternatively, have discarded them, either for good reasons, or out of forgetfulness, slackness or downright sinfulness.

For example:

1.5.85

Today's meditation was all about seeds, Christ the sower, we the seeds.

Why do I always remember the bad things that happen to my garden seeds? The ones that get eaten by mice, killed by frost, withered because I forget to water them. That kind of negative thinking won't get me far. So today, told to plant a seed, I resolved to be more positive.

Chose a sunflower seed — large and easy to grow. Remembered the plastic bag so it doesn't dry out. Put it in the airing cupboard. *Must* remember to look at it every day. *Must* get it into the light before it gets too leggy. God'll make it grow if I don't neglect it.

Do I really want God to plant some of my talents where they'll grow? Sounds too much like hard work. People aren't like sunflowers. Or are they? Does God want me to be a sunflower or a busy bee? Wish I knew. There's that negative attitude again. Lord, show me who I am.

If you like the idea of keeping a spiritual journal you can use this two month period to try it out to see if it's your kind of thing. If you don't enjoy it, just leave it alone with a good conscience.

Which Bible?

The right equipment is important to the success of any adventure. On this particular journey your bible is the most important item in your luggage and needs to be chosen carefully.

Many readers will already know a modern translation of the bible such as the Jerusalem Bible (1966), the New English Bible (1970), the Good News Bible (1966-76), the Living Bible (1971), the New American Standard Bible (1971) and the New International Version (1978). Some of you will be using one or more of these bibles for your study and devotional reading in preference to one of the older translations such as the Douay Bible (1609) and the King James Authorised Version (1611). Others will be happiest with these older versions because of the sheer beauty of the seventeenth century English language.

You may decide to take any familiar version of the bible with you on this journey. Before you do so, please consider the possible advantages of taking a different version of the bible along with you, whose language and nuances of meaning are less well known to you. Such a bible may help you to gain fresh insights into the text as it relates to your present personal circumstances. I have done that myself in the preparation of this course for I chose to use the New International Version which I had never read before. I have found it a helpful experience: moreover, when I have come across unfamiliar expressions which appear to alter the meaning of the text I've been able to compare the new reading with others in order to expand my understanding of the passage.

The texts used for the meditations are all taken from the New International Version. Have your own bible handy as well. One with cross references and a concordance can be very helpful. I've used The Open Bible, New American Standard Version, published by T. Nelson in 1979 as my chief resource bible but there are others you might prefer to use. It is worth looking around to find what you want.

The bible is the only book I have taken with me on this particular journey. It's the only book I read every single day, even if I have time for only a few verses. It has nourished my spirit as much as good food has nourished my body. I feel as hungry if I neglect to read my bible as I do if I fast from food for any length of time.

You're just about ready to start the program now, but, before you start, there's just one more thing to do. You need to take a cool look at your present state of fitness.

WHAT DOES IT TAKE TO BE SPIRITUALLY FIT?

Fitness is not easy to define. It's a condition which is certainly accompanied by a sense of physical well being, mental agility and emotional contentment. It certainly involves being in tune with one's environment. Many people, including myself, would add that fitness also involves being at peace with God and one's neighbours. Our health, in the Christian view, depends upon our having a right relationship with God.

God has established the possibility of that relationship through the enfleshing of Jesus Christ and his atoning work performed on the cross. Our part in that work is to 'rejoice in God through our Lord Jesus Christ, through whom we have now received reconciliation'. (Rom 5:11)

Repentence is part of our rejoicing. So too are sacrifice and service. If we are to know what it means to have a right relationship with God we must take Christian discipleship seriously. We need the nourishment we can get from Bible reading, corporate worship, individual prayer and service to our neighbours. We cannot 'go it alone'. God gives us many means of building on the foundations given to us when we received the gift of faith.

There have been times in my own life when repentance has been easy, solutions to problems have been obvious and discipleship has been a daily joy. There have been other times when life has been very different and I have felt that I have lost my way and am condemned to life in a thick fog for the rest of my life. Then discipleship has been a real struggle. At such times I have found it a great help to have a very simple 'rule' of life to follow a daily discipline like the one monks use. This keeps me close to God even when I feel a thousand miles apart. For myself that rule has consisted in saying the prayer Christ taught us to say each day, opening my bible once a day to read God's word, going to church each week whatever I feel like, and saying a kind word to someone each day. 'Church' hasn't always meant going inside a building. It can mean being with other Christians in a small group, singing, talking and praying with each other. 'Going to Church' means seeking fellowship with other Christians. Keeping a rule is one way of giving the Holy Spirit a chance, of saying 'yes' to God even when you feel like saying 'no'. My own rule is minimal, basic and simple. It may not suit your own situation. Each of us needs to work out a way of discipleship.

If our spiritual health depended on our own efforts we should soon fall sick. It does not. 'God heals, I bandage', said that great seventeenth century surgeon, Ambrose Paré. He got his priorities right, and so must we. Our spiritual exercises can be thought of as stepping stones or bandages, depending on our mood, but it is God who leads us safely across the river. It is God alone who heals us.

Personal relationships

Creative relationships are essential to good emotional health. This doesn't mean that you should expect to be happy all the time, or get your own way over everything. It does mean that you and I need to take the Sermon on the Mount as our guide book for life. The ideals which should govern all our relationships are laid down there. Although we know we are unlikely to be able to live up to those ideals we can at least try. In trying, we shall discover each other. The fourth week of the exercises is given over to a study of some of the precepts given to us by Christ in the Sermon on the Mount. Here, I only want to point to that dialogue between Jesus and an expert in mosaic law which preceded the parable of the Good Samaritan:

'On one occasion an expert in the law stood up to test Jesus. "Teacher", he asked, "what must I do to inherit eternal life?"

"What is written in the Law?" he replied. "How do you read it?"

He answered: "Love the Lord your God with all your heart and with all your soul and with all your strength and with all your mind; and, 'Love your neighbour as yourself.'

"You have answered correctly," Jesus replied.

"Do this and you will live." (Luke 10:25-28)

"All the law and the prophets hang on these two commandments."' (Matt 22:40)

Loving our neighbour and ourselves is a lifetime's work, not something that we will be able to accomplish in the space of two months. However, it can be good to choose one aspect of your personal relationships that you feel could do with a bit of improvement. With the help of a friend you could look at practical ways of doing this and so try to help the Holy Spirit to accomplish God's work in your life.

Physical exercise

This book is a challenge to the attitude to physical exercise which is promoted by fasionable work-out books. It is not a challenge to physical exercise itself. Far from it. A modest amount of exercise every day is vital to our physical, emotional and spiritual health. Most of us who do sedentary work and drive cars need to take regular physical exercise to keep ourselves fit.

There are lots of enjoyable and companionable ways of taking exercise. Choose what you want to do and enjoy yourself. There is a marvellous quotation from the Bible which should govern your approach to exercise:

'He gives strength to the weary
and increases the power of the weak.
Even youths grow tired and weary,
and young men stumble, and fall;
but those who hope in the Lord
will renew their strength.
They will soar on wings like eagles;
they will run and not grow weary,
They will walk and not faint.'
                Isa 40:29-31)

Diet

Diet is becoming a matter of considerable importance as it is now widely accepted that many diseases and emotional disorders, particularly in children and young people, are related to food intake. Malnutrition of various kinds, excess food, dietary imbalance, food intolerances and allergies and chemical pollution of food by colourants and other additives have all been implicated in the causing of malaise and serious ill health.

These links between food and illnesses can be well established in individuals. Scientific papers about them are published frequently and make interesting reading. Cures abound. Hard facts are not easy to come by. 'One man's meat is another man's poison', is a good adage to hold on to whenever you find yourself being swayed by passionate appeals to you to adopt a particular diet or buy a particular product which is alleged to be a panacea for all ills.

Food is a fascinating subject. I could easily fill these pages with my own pet theories, my experiments with all kinds of diets, mainly for slimming, and my failures to stick to any of them for any length of time. I should have to say, 'do as I say and not as I do' as a prelude to any advice I might offer. In the end I would have to admit that I might be wrong. So I am not going to say 'you must' or 'you must not' about anything. Instead, I would suggest that you take certain phrases in the Bible very seriously.

'Man does not live on bread alone, but on every word that comes from the mouth of God.' (Matt 4:4.)

'Give us today our daily bread.' (Matt 6:11.)

'Which of you, if his son asks for bread, will give him a stone?' (Matt 7:9.)

'And if anyone gives even a cup of cold water to one of these little ones because he is my disciple, I will tell you the truth, he will certainly not lose his reward.' (Matt 10:42.)

'Do not be deceived: God cannot be mocked. A man reaps what he sows.' (Gal 6:7.)

'Be very careful then, how you live – not as unwise but as wise, making the most of every opportunity, because the days are evil. Therefore do not be foolish, but understand what the Lord's will is. Do not get drunk on wine which leads to debauchery. Instead be filled with the Spirit.' (Eph 5:15-18.)

To these, I would simply add one modern saying:

'Live simply, that others may simply live.'

Whenever we eat anything at all we eat another creature's life. This is true whether we are meat eaters, vegetarians or vegans. Their life is sacrificed in order that we may live. When I became a vegetarian I was glad to be able to give up taking the lives of animals but then I became increasingly aware of the life I was consuming in large quantities when I ate vegetables and fruits. This has brought me closer to my meat-eating family and friends again, and helped me to reverence the life I have taken in order to stay alive myself.

If, then, you are reverent about the things you eat, moderate in your appetites, aware of the needs of others and of the joy of sharing what you have with those who have less, you will, I think, find that you enjoy your own food more and grow more healthy. In matters of food, of physical exercise and of relationships with others keep yourself aware that you are dealing with God's creation, and that in order to be spiritually fit, indeed in order to be fit in all aspects of your being, you must act in accord with God plan for that creation.

WEEK ONE – CALL TO ADVENTURE

'In all the travels of the Israelites, whenever
the cloud lifted from above the tabernacle,
they would set out; but if the cloud did not
lift, they did not set out – until the day it
lifted.'

Ex 40: 36-7

'Whoever serves me must follow me; and
where I am, my servant also will be.''

Jn 12:20

'This then is how you should pray:
  "'Our Father in heaven,
  hallowed be your name,
  your kingdom come,
  your will be done
  on earth as it is in heaven.
  Give us today our daily bread.
  Forgive us our debts,
  as we also have forgiven our debtors.
  And lead us not into temptation,
  but deliver us from the evil one."''

Matt 6:9-13

WEEK ONE – CALL TO ADVENTURE

Act of Commitment

As you test your physical strength, ask God to grant you spiritual health.

Position: lying on the floor, flat on your back, hands by your side, palms on floor.

- Keep your feet on the floor. Tighten stomach muscles. Lift head off floor; then lower it to count of 4. Rest for count of 4 (repeat 4 times).
- Lift left leg off floor, keeping knee straight. Raise leg to right angle, pointing toes, to count of 4. Lower to count of 4 (repeat 4 times).
- Repeat (2) with right leg.

- Tighten your stomach muscles and press back on to floor. Then raise both legs to right angle at once to count of 4 and lower to count of 4. (repeat twice).
- From starting position, extend both arms out sideways, sweeping floor with palms till they meet above your head. Do this to count of 4. Lock thumbs together; stretch upwards for count of 4. Return hands to side to count of 4 (repeat 4 times).
- Hands by your side, stomach tight, raise both legs high above your head. Then swing them down and sit up in one swift movement. Lie down slowly to count of 4 (repeat twice).

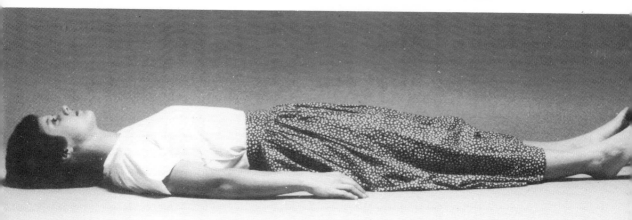

Centering down

Position: Sitting on the floor cross-legged.

Sit up tall. Shut your eyes. Take a deep breath in; as you do this, say *'Jesus'* quietly to yourself. Breathe out slowly, saying, *'My Lord and my God.'*

Repeat this phrase gently and quietly in rhythm with your quiet deep breathing until you feel still and collected in yourself.

Prayer for a meeting

As soon as you are still, say the Lord's prayer slowly.

Meditation

Equipment: a single seed of any kind.

Take your seed into your hand. Close your eyes. Feel the seed's shape, size, hardness, weight.

Picture what this seed could become. Picture what might happen to it. Read aloud:

'A farmer went out to sow his seed. As he was scattering the seed, some fell along the path, and the birds came and ate it up. Some fell on rocky places, where it did not have much soil. It sprang up quickly, because the soil was shallow. But when the sun came up, the plants were scorched, and they withered because they had no root. Other seed fell among thorns, which grew up and choked the plants. Still other seed fell on good soil, where it produced a crop – a hundred, sixty or thirty times what was sown. He who has ears, let him hear.' (Matt 13: 3b-9.)

God has sown seed in you. What will happen to it? How will you nourish it?

Action for the day: Take the seed in your hand and put it somewhere. Note what you have done with it.

Later reflection

Relax in your comfortable chair. Close your eyes and center down, using the Jesus prayer to help you.

Open your bible and read the parable of the sower in Matthew 13: 1-30.

What chance did you give your seed today? What will you have to do for it to grow and flower, or bear fruit?

What chance have you given God's word today?

In your journal write down one thing you will have to do for your planted seed if it is to grow. What is the spiritual equivalent of that action? Write that down, too.

Act of Commitment

As you enjoy your freedom to move ask God to free you from the chains of sin.

Position: standing upright, arms by your side, fingers pointed.

- Circle left arm from shoulder, making wide, vigorous movement to count of 6. Rest for 2 counts (repeat 6 times).
- Repeat with right arm.
- Repeat using both arms.
- Stand on right leg, foot turned slightly outwards, raise left leg sideways, toes pointed backwards. Kick high to count of 2. Return to standing. Count 2 (repeat 4 times).
- Repeat standing on left leg and kicking with right.
- Standing on both feet, extend both arms sideways and upwards over your head, to count of 4. Lock thumbs, rise to tip toe, hold position for 4 counts. Lower to standing, return arms to side to count of 4. Rest for 4 counts (repeat 4 times).
- Touch your toes with both hands, fingers pointed. Make loose fists and drop forwards on to knuckles, slightly reaching forwards, keeping knees straight and toes on ground. Push off ground and stand up. Do this to count of 8 in all (repeat 4 times).

Centering down

Position: sitting on the floor cross-legged. Hold your han lightly in your lap so that yo can use your fingers to cou your breaths.

Take 10 deep slow breaths, saying under your breath, *Jesus, free me from my cha*

Prayer for a meeting

Close your eyes, center on the word *Jesus*. See yourself running forwards to meet him, free from all that enslaves you, free to follow him.

Meditation

Equipment: three stones of any kind.

Take one of the stones into your hand. Close your eyes; feel its weight. Imagine that weight multiplied a thousandfold, in a sack on your back, or in a case, yourself hurrying to catch a train. You are late. How will you catch that train?

Read aloud:

> 'As Jesus was walking beside the Sea of Galilee, he saw two brothers, Simon called Peter and his brother Andrew. They were casting a net into the lake, for they were fishermen. "Come, follow me," Jesus said, "and I will make you fishers of men." At once they left their nets and followed him.' (Matt 4: 18-20.)

Take the other two stones into your hands. Ask God to show you three things they represent:

- a possession, like nets, which you could leave behind for the next 2 months.
- a particular sin that weighs you down.
- an attitude, not sinful in itself, which may be hampering you from following Jesus.

Action for the day: put the 3 stones in your pocket. Carry them with you all day. If you have no pockets, tie them in a bag and string them round your neck. It's important to have them on your person.

Later reflection

Relax in a comfortable chair. Center down.

Think about your stones. Do you think you chose the right possession, sin and attitude to leave behind you for the next 2 months? Be realistic. Choose little things.

In your journal write about your final choices, so that later on you can look back and see what happened.

Act of Commitment

Tighten your stomach muscles and think about the meaning of hunger.

Position: lying flat on your back, arms by your side, palms pressed on floor.

- Pull your toes up to right angle with heels. Pull your stomach muscles in tight. Hold for count of 4. Relax to count of 4 (repeat 8 times: total count 64).

- Separate legs slightly and bend your knees so that both feet are flat on floor. Raise buttocks off the floor. Hold yourself on your feet, and shoulders for count of 4. Lower buttocks. Rest to count of 4 (repeat 8 times).

- From position above roll back on to your shoulders, kicking legs and buttocks into air. (Put your clenched fists under your buttocks if you're older or not fit.) Cycle your legs vigorously 10 times. Rest: (repeat twice).

- From second cycling, cross your legs while still in the air. Roll forwards and sit up so that you end up cross-legged and tall-backed. (Stand up in one movement if you are already fit.)

- Repeat above.

Centering down

Position: kneeling, resting bottom on heels, or use a prayer stool to rest your body off your heels.

Settle into relaxed position, hands resting lightly on your knees, palms open and upward.

Slow and deepen your breathing for 10 breaths.

Try to feel empty and hungry for food. Bring your hands together, one palm supporting the back of the other hand. Raise them as if to plead for food.

Prayer for a meeting

When you are centered, kneel upright, hands extended. God, who loves you, will give you what you need today. So, be still and pray: *Abba, hear my prayer.* Amen.

Meditation

Equipment: Your jar with flour and salt; small jug of oil; water in jug; small bowl; plate. (Bible)

Transfer nearly all flour to bowl. Feel and taste flour, oil and water. Picture their origins and the work that turned raw materials into your food.

Do you remember the story of Elijah and the woman of Zarephath? He was hungry and asked her for bread. Read on aloud:

> '"As surely as the Lord your God lives," she replied, "I don't have any bread – only à handful of flour in a jar and a little oil in a jug. I am gathering a few sticks to take home and make a meal for myself and my son, that we may eat it – and die.
>
> Elijah said to her, "Don't be afraid. Go home and do as you have said. But first make a small cake of bread for me from what you have and bring it to me, and then make something for yourself and your son."' (1 Kings 17: 12-13.)

She did, and the story has a happy ending as you can read for yourself if you wish.

Mix the flour, oil and water into a kneadable dough. Use the left-over flour to flatten it into a pancake (chapatti) in your hands. Think of all the places in the world where such food is cooked and shared every day.

Action for the day: cook your 'cake' in a greased frying pan. Wrap in greaseproof paper. Who will you share it with?

Later reflection

Relax. Center down.

Did you share your food today? With whom? How was your gift received?

In your journal write about what happened to your feelings during and after the exercise. Try to be honest with yourself. Write about the person you shared with.

...t of Commitment

...by life's natural rhythms of work and
...

...sition: standing upright, feet together,
...nds by your side, palms open and
...ing forwards.

...Swing both arms sideways and
...upwards to brisk count of 2. Clap
...hands and return to sides to count of
...2. Rest to count of 2 (repeat 4 times).
...Keeping arms still, jump to feet
...apart, then to feet-together position
...o brisk count of 2. Rest to count of 2
...repeat 4 times).
...Put the above two steps together so
...hat when you bring your arms
...sideways to clap above your head
...you are also jumping into legs-apart
...position, and vice versa. Remember
...to rest to count of 2 between jumps
...repeat 4 times).
...Rest for 8 to 16 counts, depending on
...fitness.
...Repeat above four steps 2-4 times
...depending on fitness.
...Stand tall. Raise both arms sideways
...and bring above head as if to receive
...something from above you. Do this to
...count of 4. Look up. Rise to tiptoe
...position. Hold to count of 4 (repeat 4
...imes).

...entering down

...sition: standing upright. Stand easy,
... alert.

...ut your eyes and focus your attention
... your breathing. Empty your mind of
...f-centered thoughts. When you are
...l, reach upwards as in the last step
...d wait expectantly to receive what
...d wants to give you. If you find it
...ficult to get still, use the word God, in
...whisper on each breath you take in, to
...p you.

Prayer for a meeting

Remain standing with hands clasped lightly at waist level. God has given you what you need for today. Thank God. When you have said what you want to say add: *All that I have, you have given me. Help me to share your gifts with others.*

Meditation

Equipment: a jug full of water and an empty glass.

This meditation is made standing. You may find it difficult to think prayerfully in this position. Please, persevere.

Put glass on floor. Pour water from jug into it. Leave glass on floor. Stand up.

You are like that glass, waiting to be filled, empty, full of nothingness. Do you remember how Jeremiah felt when God asked him to be a prophet? Read aloud how Jeremiah replied:

> '"Ah, Sovereign Lord," I said, "I do not know how to speak; I am only a child." But the Lord said to me, "Do not say, 'I am only a child.' You must go to everyone I send you to and say whatever I command you. Do not be afraid of them, for I am with you and will rescue you," declares the Lord.' (Jer 1: 6-8.)

Jeremiah felt inadequate, yet God called him.

What talents has God given you to use? Would it be right for you to pray to be given more?

Action for the day: Stoop, kneel and drink from the glass.

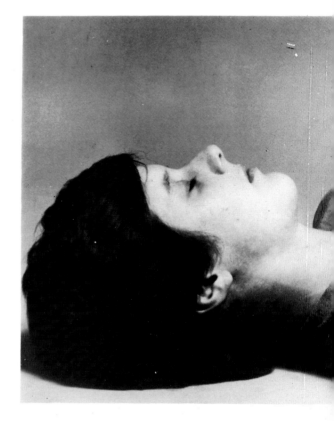

Later reflection

Relax, lying on the floor. Close your eyes and center your mind on God.

Think about that water in the glass. Did you drain the glass? Did you replenish it from the jug? Could you have shared it?

How have you used God's gifts to you today?

In your journal note down any talent you have which God might wish to use, nurture and expand. Describe what standing, stooping and kneeling said to your soul and spirit.

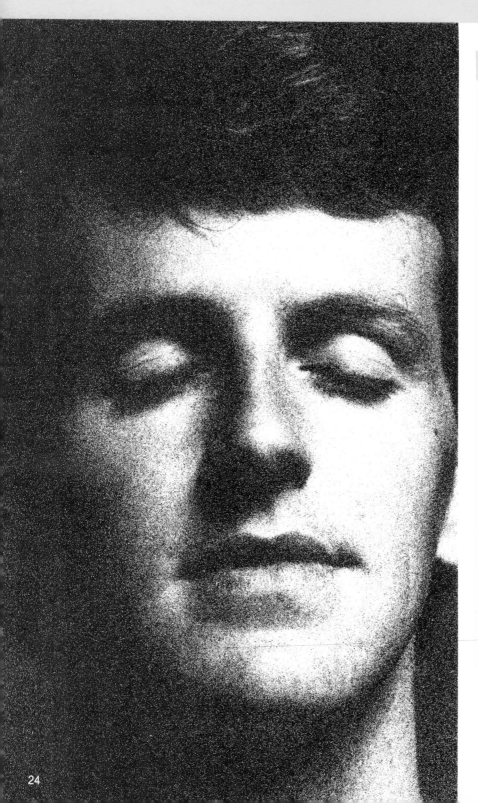

Act of Commitment

As you reach out with your body, let your mind reach out to a friend.

Position: standing upright, feet together, hands by side

- Raise both arms out sideways and sweep them overhead. Lock thumbs; then return arms to side. All to count of 8 (repeat 4 times).
- Extend arms overhead as above. Lock thumbs, point fingers, bend and touch toes. Return to starting position. All to count of 8 (repeat 4 times).
- Lean body sideways to left; slide left hand down left leg to touch calf. Stand up and repeat to right. All to count of 8 (repeat 4 times).
- Separate feet slightly. Extend arms sideways to shoulder height. Swing and twist body to left; sweep round to right as far as you can go. Count of 8 (repeat 4 times).
- Keeping buttocks well tucked in, step forwards with left leg; lean weight on that leg, sweep right hand forwards as if to shake hands; step back. All to count of 8 (repeat 4 times).
- Repeat last step stepping on to right leg.
- Repeat all steps once or twice according to time.

Centering down

Position: sitting upright on hard-backed chair or stool, hands on your lap to use fingers for counting.

Shut your eyes. Focus attention on breathing. Take 10 deep slow breaths. Empty your mind, using the *Jesus* prayer to help you if necessary.

After 10 breaths allow yourself to be utterly still without movement or thought of any kind. Hold this stillness at the beginning and end of each deep breath till you feel quiet in the whole of yourself.

Prayer for a meeting

Remain sitting, hands lightly clasped to count with fingers. Pray for 5 people you can call friends or would like to be friendly with. Do this in your own way or saying, *'Lord, take care of my friend...'*

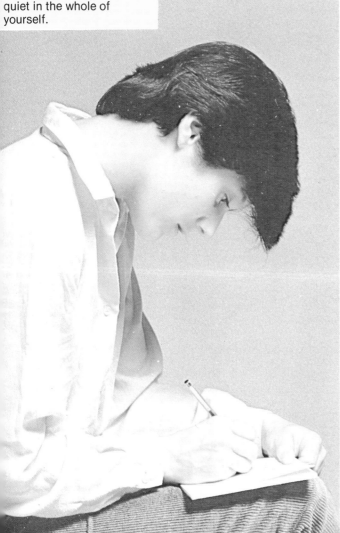

Meditation

Equipment: notebook and a pen.

This meditation is made through prayerful thought and writing. It may feel different from the kind where you shut your eyes and think and pray.

First, shut your eyes, picture one of the five. Then write his or her name down. Repeat with each.

Read aloud:

'Going on from there, Jesus saw two other brothers, James son of Zebedee and his brother John. They were in a boat with their father Zebedee, preparing their nets. Jesus called them and immediately they left the boat and their father and followed him.' (Matt 4: 21-22.)

Look again at your list. Have you included any relatives? Are all your friends human?

Did your list include anyone you would call friend, but who would not call you friend?

Note the names of 3 people outside your list who need a friend, whom you might take a step towards.

Action for the day: write down the name of one person you intend to contact today.

Later reflection

Relax in your comfortable chair. Center yourself, using the words, *Jesus, my Lord and my friend* to help.

Think about the 5 friends you prayed for today.

Did you reach out to that other person today? Did anyone reach out to you? How, and what happened?

In your journal note the name of anyone whom you did not like initially but who has now become a friend. Describe how it happened.

If nothing like that has ever happened to you, describe the beginning of any friendship, and say how you think friendships happen.

Act of Commitment

Let this tiny cross of discomfort remind you of Christ's great cross of suffering.

Position: lying on the floor prone, elbows bent, hands under head, palms on floor.

- Pressing down on floor with hands, lift head and shoulders off floor slowly; then lower. Total count of 8 (repeat 4 times).
- Place hands flat on floor at shoulder level. Tuck toes under, raise body into 'press up' position. Hold to count of 8. Lower yourself. Rest to count of 8 (repeat 4 times).
- Resume starting position. Repeat first two steps twice (3 times if fit).
- Get up and stand erect. Circle arms from shoulders 8 times. Then fling them into shape of a cross and hold position. Settle into slow breathing. Count breaths. Note number when your arms begin to feel heavy, and number when you want to stop. Stop when time is up.

Centering down

Position: Kneeling on floor, straight backed. You may find it a help to hold a home-made cross which you have made yourself from wood, twigs, straw or cardboard

Holding cross in your hands, or mind's eye, shut your eyes and visualise Jesus on the cross. Let the image carry you towards stillness.

If you do not find this easy use His words, *'I, if be lifted up will draw all men unto me,'* to draw you into the stillness where you can adore.

Meditation

Equipment: three coins of equal value, a sum of money to match that, your home-made cross.

Put cross on floor. Place 3 coins on its left, other money on right. What is the connection between money and sacrifice?

Read aloud:

> 'Then Jesus said to his disciples, "If anyone would come after me, he must deny himself and take up his cross and follow me. For whoever wants to save his life will lose it, but whoever loses his life for me will find it."' (Matt 16: 24-25.)

The 3 coins, whatever their value, are what you're invited to use on yourself today, as an act of disciplined love.

Ask God to show you how to spend them. Large in value, or small, they are all you have to use today.

Thank God for the other money to give away.

Action for the day: put your 3 coins into a pocket or purse where they won't get mixed up with fare money etc. Put the other money into a savings box.

Prayer for a meeting

Thank God for Jesus' sacrificial love as you kneel in still adoration.

'Jesus, my Lord, I thee adore; let me love thee more and more.'

Later reflection

Relax on the floor. Center down.

Think about the money you spent today. Was it more than you usually spend on yourself? Or less? What do you usually spend it on?

Each Friday for 8 weeks you'll have an opportunity to save money for God's use. What do you think God would like you to do with it?

In your journal describe your feelings about spending money on yourself. How do guilt and pleasure mix? Is money a sign of sacrifice at all? What else do you give God?

Act of Commitment

Use this hard leg work to help you to keep yourself fit for God's services.

Position: standing upright, heels together, toes slightly apart, hands by your side.

- Rise on tiptoe. Hold balance to count of 8. Lower heels. Stand to count of 8 (repeat 8 times).
- Rise slightly, bend knees into deep curtsey and squat to count of 4. Rise to count of 4 (repeat 8 times).
- Stand on left leg. Bring right leg with bent knee to chest level. Grip tight to body with hands. Hold to count of 4. Return to stand (repeat 4 times).
- Repeat last step standing on right leg and raising left.
- Repeat all four steps once.
- Mark time, starting slowly, then breaking into vigorous running on the spot. Run hard for the remainder of your 4 minutes.

Centering down

Position: kneeling upright on the floor with your hands lightly clasped in front of you.

You have been running hard. Wait quietly till your breathing slows naturally and you feel your pulse slow.

Allow yourself to flow into the rhythm. Still your conscious thoughts. Allow the rhythm to take you beyond thought.

Open your arms wide as if you were going to greet a beloved friend.

Prayer for a meeting

Kneeling upright, with your arms open to the future, invite Jesus to be your guest today, praying with confidence: *'Even so, come Lord Jesus.'*

Meditation

Equipment: plasticine or other modelling material.

God invites us to share in the shaping of our lives through the gift of free will. If we give ourselves to God we shall be shaped by God.

Jeremiah was told by God to watch a potter:

'So I went down to the potter's house, and I saw him working at the wheel. But the pot he was shaping from the clay was marred in his hands; so the potter formed it into another pot, shaping it as seemed best to him.

Then the word of the Lord came to me: "O house of Israel, can I not do with you as this potter does?" declares the Lord. "Like clay in the hand of the potter, so are you in my hand, O house of Israel."' (Jer 18: 3-6.)

Take your 'clay' in your hands. Ask God to use your hands as you shape it into something new. As you work do not think about making something like a work of art; just allow your fingers freedom to be God's tools.

How might God want to reshape your life?

Action for the day: when you have made the shape you feel satisfied with, put it into a safe place for the day.

Later reflection

Relax in your comfortable chair, having put your shape somewhere visible from where you are.

Center down, using the words, *'Come Lord Jesus.'*

Do you still like your 'shape'? What is it saying to you about your own 'shape'? Can the 'clay' help the potter? How?

In your journal draw the shape you and God have made, or describe it in words.

Write down one way in which you think God might want to reshape you to fit you for your future work as a friend and follower of Jesus.

'Think of what you were when you were called. Not many of you were wise by human standards; not many were influential; not many were of noble birth. But God chose the weak things of the world to shame the strong. He chose the lowly things of this world and the despised things – and the things that are not – to nullify the things that are, so that no one may boast before him. It is because of him that you are in Christ Jesus who has become for us wisdom from God – that is our righteousness, holiness and redemption. Therefore, as it is written: "Let him who boasts, boast in the Lord."'

1 Cor 1:26-31.

THE JOURNEY ITSELF

WEEK TWO – SETTING OUT

'The Lord had said to Abram,
"Leave your country, your people
and your father's household and go to the
land I will show you."'

Gen 12:1.

'Come let us go up to the mountain of
the Lord,
to the house of the God of Jacob.
He will teach us his ways, so that we may walk
in his paths.'

Isa 2:3.

'Still another said, "I will follow you, Lord;
but first let me go back and say good-bye to
my family." Jesus replied, "No-one who
puts his hand to the plough and looks back
is fit for service in the kingdom of God."'

Luke 9:61-62.

Act of Commitment

Let this physical work prepare your body for its spiritual work.

Position: lying flat on your back, toes pointed, arms by your side, palms on floor.

- Flex left foot, lifting heel slightly off floor. Feel the pull on your calf. Hold to count of 4. Return to pointed toes (repeat 4 times).
- Repeat above with right foot.
- Pull stomach muscles in, repeat first step using both feet at once.
- Sit up with straight back, leaning slightly back on extended arms. Flex left foot. Press left knee into floor to tighten thigh muscles. Hold tight for count of 4. Relax (repeat 4 times).
- Repeat last step with right foot and leg.
- Repeat with both legs at once.
- Lie down flat again; starting position. Spread both legs widely apart. Feel pull on inner thigh muscles. Hold to count of 4. Close feet (repeat 4 times).
- Pull stomach muscles in tight. Flex both feet, tighten all leg muscles and try to sit up. Fold arms if you know you can. Otherwise lean on elbows slightly to gain leverage.
- Repeat all exercises twice (3-4 times if fit).

Centering down

Position: sitting up on floor, straight backed, toes pointed.

Tighten your buttock muscles; make your body tall, breathing in as you do so. Relax as you breathe out (repeat 3 times).

Imagine yourself walking along a road. You see a hill ahead. Take a deep breath and say to yourself, *'Come, let us go up to the mountain of the Lord.'*

...ayer for a meeting

...nd up. Close your eyes. Imagine ...'re at the foot of a steep hill. Ask ...d for help: *'Strengthen me, O God, for ...s journey.'*

...editation

...uipment: a pair of socks and shoes.

...on a chair with bare feet. Have your ...ks and shoes ready to put on.

...our body ready for a journey? Do you ...l fit? Probably not, but with God's ...p you'll set out. Is it worth making a ...onnoitre?

...ad how Joshua went about surveying ...known land that needed alloting to ...en Israelite tribes:

...So Joshua said to the Israelites: ...How long will you wait before you ...egin to take possession of the land ...at the Lord, the God of your fathers, ...as given you? Appoint three men ...om each tribe. I will send them out ...o make a survey of the land and to ...rite a description of it, according to ...ne inheritance of each. Then they will ...eturn to me."' (Josh 18: 3-4.)

...en was the last time you went out to ...v the land? For a new house, a new ..., a special holiday? Or a new ...ristian community? Did you prepare ...urself? What did you look for? Was ...e venture a success? What did you ...rn?

...ion for the day: put on your socks ...d shoes. Let today be a journey. ...epare to make a survey.

...ter reflection

...lax in your comfortable chair. Close ...ir eyes. Center down.

...member today. What did you notice ...out it? Whom did you meet? What did ...u learn? Will today have any relation ...tomorrow?

...your journal describe one fragment of ...ay's journey. Choose the first ...ment that comes into your mind. ...en you have made your description, ...e if it has any bearing on tomorrow.

Act of Commitment

As you exercise ask God to show you how to share other people's burdens.

Position: kneeling on the floor, sitting back on your heels, hands resting lightly on your knees.

- Pull your body up till it feels tall. Kneel up slowly, keeping spine straight, shoulders well back. Do this to count of 4. Hold upright kneeling to 8. Sit slowly back on heels and hold. Count of 8 (repeat 4 times).
- Cross your arms at chest level. Tuck chin in; curl your whole body slowly forwards into a ball till forehead rests on floor. Do this to count of 8. Rest for 8 counts. Uncurl slowly from stomach, vertebra by vertebra, head up last, to count of 8. Rest 8 (repeat 4 times).
- Kneel upright slowly; then rise to stand tall. Brace shoulders back vigorously 8 times.
- Shrug shoulders up and down briskly 8 times.
- Stand with feet together, keeping back straight, bottom well tucked in, kneel slowly and sit back on your heels again. Do to slow count of 8.
- Repeat all steps once only. This is a slow exercise. If you're not fit, it may make you feel a little dizzy. If so, tuck stomach in tight and dc once only.

Centering down

Position: kneeling on floor, sitting back on your heels; or body on stool ledge.

Close your eyes. Put your chin on your chest. Cover your eyes with cupped hands. Allow yourself to swim into the warm darkness.

Slow and deepen your breathing. Empty your mind and wait on God. If it is difficult to empty your mind focus your thoughts and whisper: *'He made darkness His covering, His canopy around Him'.* (Ps 18: 11)

Prayer for a meeting

Look into the darkness. There's a journey ahead. Pray for God's help: *'All my trust is in Thee, O God.'*

Meditation

Equipment: one small stone.

Hold your stone. Close your eyes. Remember last week's three sto Could one of them still hamper your journey?

Read what Jesus said to his disciples when he sent them out to p and to heal:

'He told them: "Take nothing for the journey – no staff, no bag, r no money, no extra tunic. Whatever house you enter, stay there leave the town. If people do not welcome you, shake the dust of feet when you leave their town as a testimony against them." Sc set out and went from village to village, preaching the gospel an healing people everywhere.' (Luke 9: 3-6.)

Some followers of Jesus are still called to that kind of trusting. Mc are not. But we can at least discard surplus baggage and learn to little.

Ask God to show you the truth about those 3 'stones'. Are any stil Or have you picked up another?

Action for the day: take your stone out of doors. Hurl it away safel do so, ask God to fill the gap with trust.

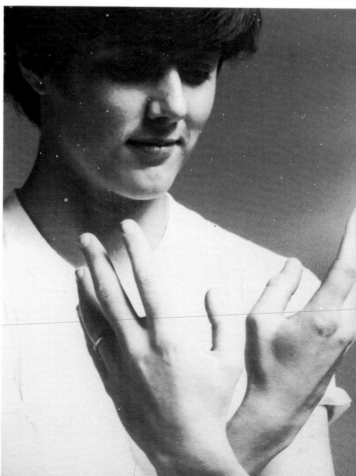

Later reflection

Relax in your comfortable chair. Close your eyes; center yourself in the warm darkness.

Remember today's real journey. How have you trusted God to supply your needs today?

In your journal write down one way you feel you could trust God to supply your needs tomorrow. Find a prayer about trust, or compose one yourself, and enter it in your journal.

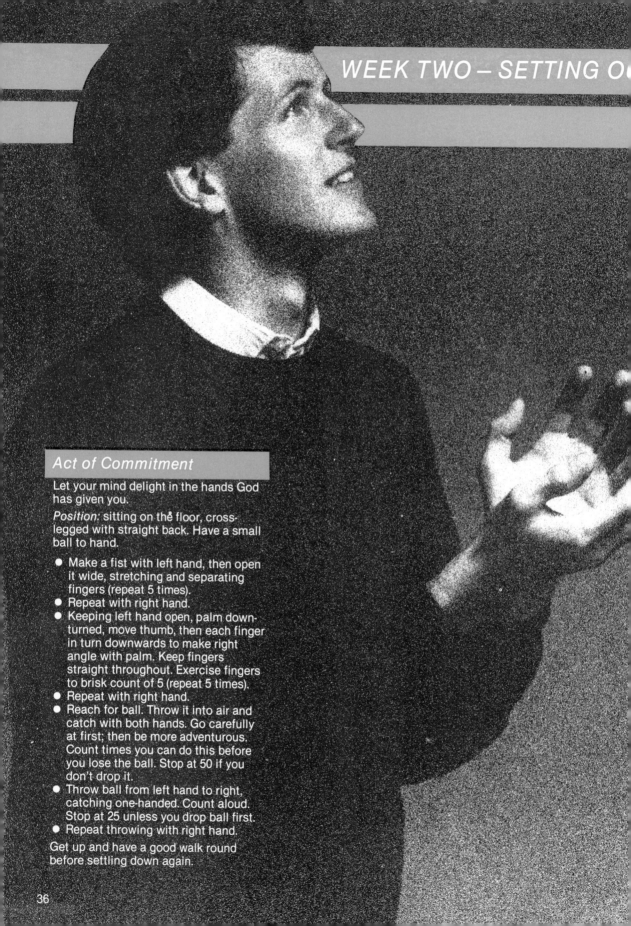

Act of Commitment

Let your mind delight in the hands God has given you.

Position: sitting on the floor, cross-legged with straight back. Have a small ball to hand.

- Make a fist with left hand, then open it wide, stretching and separating fingers (repeat 5 times).
- Repeat with right hand.
- Keeping left hand open, palm down-turned, move thumb, then each finger in turn downwards to make right angle with palm. Keep fingers straight throughout. Exercise fingers to brisk count of 5 (repeat 5 times).
- Repeat with right hand.
- Reach for ball. Throw it into air and catch with both hands. Go carefully at first; then be more adventurous. Count times you can do this before you lose the ball. Stop at 50 if you don't drop it.
- Throw ball from left hand to right, catching one-handed. Count aloud. Stop at 25 unless you drop ball first.
- Repeat throwing with right hand.

Get up and have a good walk round before settling down again.

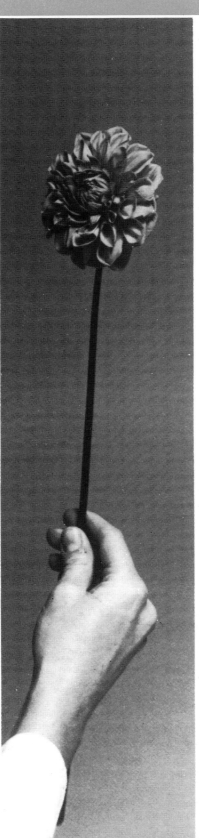

Centering down

Position: sitting cross-legged on floor or cushion, hands folded lightly on your lap.

Close your eyes. Slow your breathing. Drop your shoulders. Relax deeply, chin on chest, but back straight.

Imagine the blood flowing from your heart to your finger tips and toes.

Find your pulse just above your left thumb. Feel it. Rejoice in the vigour of your life.

Prayer for a meeting

As you become aware of your pulse, become aware also of your dependence on God for every moment of your life. Give thanks to God for this gift.

Meditation

Equipment: a flower, or a picture of one.

Place your flower or picture where you can see it from where you are sitting. Look at it. Allow its beauty to nourish you.

The flower is God's gift to you today. How will you receive it? What will you do with it? What is your attitude towards giving and receiving?

Read what Jesus says to his followers:

> '"Be merciful, just as your Father is merciful. Do not judge, and you will not be judged. Do not condemn, and you will not be condemned. Forgive, and you will be forgiven. Give and it will be given to you. A good measure, pressed down, shaken together and running over, will be poured into your lap. For with the measure you use, it will be measured to you."' (Luke 6: 36-38.)

Are you as generous to others as God is to you? Can you receive what God and others give you?

Action for the day: keep your flower but find something else you would like to share with one other person.

Later reflection

Put your flower where you can see it from your comfortable chair. Relax and center yourself by enjoying the beauty of God's gift to you.

Did anyone give you a gift today? Did you give anyone a gift today? How was that sharing?

In your journal describe one occasion when you were given something and one when you gave something. Were those occasions of true sharing? What does sharing mean?

Act of Commitment

Ask God to help you to tread out the way of holiness.

Position: standing upright.

- Mark time at walking pace to count of 8.
- Break into trot and mark time to count of 8.
- With feet together leap as high as you can into the air (repeat 8 times).
- Jump in feet apart, feet together rhythm (repeat 8 times).
- With feet together, jump to left. Return to centre (repeat 8 times).
- Repeat to right.
- With feet together, jump forwards. Jump round to face in reverse. Jump back to start. Turn (repeat 8 times).
- Repeat all above steps at a vigorous pace until your 4 minutes is up.

Centering down

Position: Go for a short walk, up and down your room, or outside in the fresh air, for about three minutes.

Just enjoy the feel of your movements, the swing of your arms, the spring in your feet.

Then return to the place where you want to pray and meditate. Settle yourself into the position you find most comfortable for prayer and thought.

Prayer for a meeting

As soon as you are still, thank God for your body. Pray for guidance for the next part of your journey. *'Show me Your ways, O Lord: teach me Your paths.'*

Meditation

Equipment: your working notebook; a pen or pencil.

Draw yourself a road. Put in a signpost at the beginning. Write in your destination.

Is your road straight? Does it end? Read Isaiah's ideas:

'And a highway will be there;
    it will be called the Way of
                        Holiness.
The unclean will not journey on it;
    It will be for those who walk in that
                        Way;
    wicked fools will not go about on it.
No lion will be there,
    nor will any ferocious beast get up
                        on it;
    they will not be found there.
But only the redeemed will walk there,
    and the ransomed of the Lord will
                        return."
                        (Isa 35: 8-9.)

You have already travelled a little way on the highway of Holiness.

How does God protect and help you as you walk in that Way? Write your answers in your notebook.

Action for the day: write a short prayer asking God to help you along the Way. Try to make it simple so that you can recall it whenever you want to use it.

Later reflection

Relax. Close your eyes. Center down. Then say the Lord's prayer as an act of devotion.

Recall your day. How did God protect and help you today? Was it in ways you had thought of in the meditation?

In your journal describe the qualities of character you feel you need in order to reach the next stopping point on your journey.

Act of Commitment

Try to let everything you see, hear and touch in the next few minutes speak to you of God.

Position: sitting on chair, feet on ground, back upright and unsupported.

- Face forwards; turn head to left, then slowly swivel it backwards and over to hold right ear close to shoulder. Return to start (do to count of 8) (repeat 4 times).
- Repeat in reverse, starting by turning head to right.
- Drop head forwards so chin rests on chest. Do this to count of 4. Rest for 4 counts. Uncurl head and extend it backwards, chin high in air (repeat 4 times).
- Center head to face forwards. Moving only your eyes, look left, then make them move through an arc upwards and to right; then downwards and to left (repeat twice).
- Repeat in reverse direction, beginning by looking right.
- Hold head still. Move lower jaw from side to side, four complete times. Then open and shut mouth 4 times. Be gentle – some people have stiffer or looser jaws than others.
- Hands by your side, stand up to count of 4. Sit down again to count of 4. Rest 4 counts (repeat 4 times).
- Stand up: push chair back. Extend both arms sideways and bring overhead, to count of 4. Lock thumbs; dive to touch toes to count of 4. Uncurl slowly to count of 4 (repeat 4 times).

Centering down

Position: sitting on your hard chair, feet on ground, back straight and unsupported.

Shut your eyes and listen to the tiny noises in the room: the sound of your breathing, the ticking of a clock, the song of birds, traffic passing by, people's voices.

Allow the sounds their freedom in your mind.

Prayer for a meeting

Take a sound you heard in the quiet. Trace it to its source. Thank God for that creation and for your mind that can perceive it. Do the same with the other sounds.

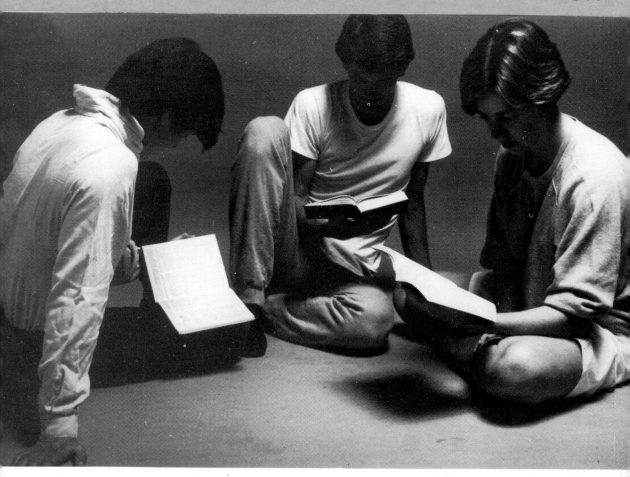

Meditation

Equipment: your bible; notebook and pen.

Use your comfortable chair for this meditation.

Open your bible at random. Allow your eyes to rest on one verse only and read it. Close your eyes and think about its meaning.

Did your verse speak to you? Did it nourish your soul, or leave you bewildered, bored or irritated?

Do you often open your Bible in that way? Or do you prefer to study systematically in a group or with a commentary to help you? Or do you do both?

Remember the story of Philip and the eunuch:

'Then Philip ran up to the chariot and heard the man reading Isaiah the prophet. "Do you understand what you are reading?," Philip asked.

"How can I," he said, "unless someone explains it to me?" So he invited Philip to come up and sit with him.' (Acts 8: 30-31.)

If you open your bible at that passage, you can read the rest of the story of the eunuch's conversion and baptism.

How do you share the Christian vision?

Action for the day: Make a list in your notebook of bible quotations, books, people and groups who have specially helped you to understand God's word.

Later reflection

Lie flat on the floor. Relax. Listen again to the sounds in your room.

Recall the list in your notebook. Pray for the people and groups who have helped you in the past.

In your journal write the name of one person who has shared a vision with you, and helped you, and say why you think that was.

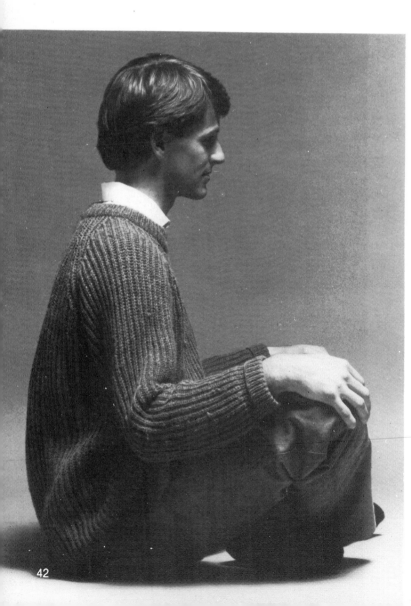

Act of Commitment

Enjoy God's world. Seek for Christ everywhere, always.

Position: standing outdoors, suitably dressed for running. Have a watch with a second hand, or a stop watch with you.

- Mark your starting point in some way.
- Walk forwards in any direction for exactly one minute.
- Turn and walk back to base. Note the time it took you to do that.
- Run forwards at an easy pace and in the same direction as the first step for exactly one minute.
- Turn and walk back to base. Note how long it took to walk back.
- When you're indoors again and ready to center down, find your notebook and pen and make a note of the difference in times it took for exercises three and five (you will need this figure later on).

Centering down

Position: sitting cross-legged on the floor, with a straight back and your hands comfortably resting on your knees.

Enjoy the feeling of well being in your body that has come to you through being outside and in charge of your bodily activities.

Now shut your eyes. Deepen your breathing and settle yourself into stillness. Empty your mind of all images if you can. If you can't yet do that, focus your attention on God through the use of the *Jesus prayer.*

Prayer for a meeting

When you are as still and empty as you can be today, allow your imagination to take you for a walk with Jesus, perhaps going up a hillside to hear him preach. Thank him for being with you now.

editation

uipment: your notebook, the smallest
in in your pocket or purse.

agine hearing that Jesus was coming
o your town or village today. Would
u be like Zaccheus?

ad aloud:

He wanted to see who Jesus was,
ut being a short man he could not,
ecause of the crowd. So he ran
ahead and climbed a sycamore-fig
ree to see him, since Jesus was
coming that way.

en Jesus reached the spot, he
ked up and said to him, "Zaccheus,
me down immediately. I must stay
your house today." So he came
wn at once and welcomed him
adly.' (Lk 19: 3-6.)

k God to show you some of the
milarities and differences between
urself and Zaccheus.

ay for the kind of humility and
termination you need to persevere in
e Christian way of life.

tion for the day: open your notebook
d find your note about (6) in your Act of
mmitment exercises. Multiply that
ure by the value of your coin. Let that
m be the amount you save today to
e away later. Put your savings away
a sacrifice of thanksgiving for your
lity to run.

Later reflection

Sit down comfortably. Relax and thank
God for our day. Remember the places
you walked to today. Did you run at all? If
so, why?

In your journal note whether you ran
today and why. For yourself? For others?
For God?

If you have not run today, describe one
incident where you ran for the sake of
God or your neighbour.

Act of Commitment

Being free to choose, choose freely.

Position: standing upright, feet slightly apart, hands on hips with elbows bent.

- Keeping legs and hips turned forwards as far as possible, twist body to left in wide swing. Give a little extra push at end. Use a count of 4. Return to original stance to count of 4 (repeat 4 times).
- Repeat, turning to right at start.
- Repeat both steps but use arms as you choose.
- Without leaning forwards or backwards, bend sideways to left, sliding hand down leg to calf. Do to count of 4. Return to upright position to count of 4 (repeat 4 times).
- Repeat bending to right.
- Keeping your hands on your hips invent an exercise you want to do, to count of 4, with your left leg (repeat 4 times).
- Repeat with right leg.
- Repeat last two steps but using hands in rhythm with legs.

Free choice is fun, but sometimes has to be worked out.

Centering down

Position: Kneel, curled into a tight ball, making yourself as small as you can.

Picture yourself as a bud, ready to burst into blossom, ready to unfold. Focus on your breathing.

Waiting is adoration; so wait. Then, very slowly, uncurl, leading with your head, until you are kneeling, sitting on your heels, ready to pray.

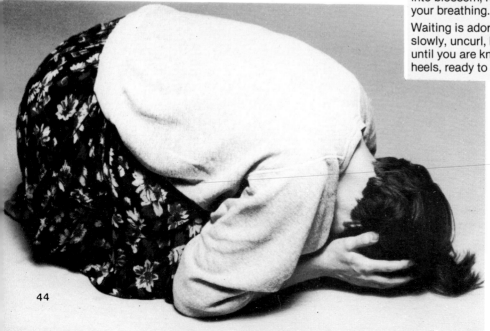

Meditation

Equipment: your notebook; a pen or pencil.

Imagine yourself walking along a road. You come to a T-junction. By chance you meet Jesus. Like the rich young ruler, you ask Jesus which way to go. Do you remember the answer?

'Jesus looked at him and loved him. "One thing you lack," he said. "Go, sell everything you have and give to the poor, and you will have treasure in heaven. Then come, follow me."

At this the man's face fell. He went away sad, because he had great wealth.' (Mark 10: 21-22.)

Try to remember a time when you had a choice rather like that ... a choice between two ways, neither evil.

Draw a T-junction in your notebook. Label the two arms of the T with your choices. Which one did you choose then? Which would you choose today?

Probably today or tomorrow you will have another choice to make. That choice will determine your future, even if your choice seems a small event. How will you approach that choice?

Action for the day: in your notebook list some of the things you would do if you were offered two jobs of equal status and pay today?

Prayer for a meeting

Thank God for the gift of free will. Pray for God's help when you have to make choices: *'Not my will, but Yours be done.'*

Later reflection

Curl up into a comfortable ball in your easy chair and relax.

Center down and thank God for your life and the freedom to make choices, however small.

What choices did you make today? Which ones will matter?

In your journal describe one choice you have made in the past which influenced the way your life has developed since then.

'But whatever was to my profit I now consider loss for the sake of Christ. What is more, I consider everything a loss compared to the surpassing greatness of knowing Christ Jesus my Lord, for whose sake I have lost all things. I consider them rubbish, that I may gain Christ and be found in him, not having a righteousness of my own that comes from the law, but that which is through faith in Christ — the righteousness that comes from God and is by faith. I want to know Christ and the power of his resurrection and the fellowship of sharing in his sufferings becoming like him in his death, and so, somehow, to attain to the resurrection from the dead.'

Phil 3: 7-11.

THE JOURNEY ITSELF

WEEK THREE – PROVISIONS FOR PILGRIMS

'Remember how the Lord your God led you
all the way in the desert these forty years, to
humble you and to test you in order to know
what was in your heart, whether or not you
would keep his commands. He humbled
you, causing you to hunger and then feeding
you with manna, which neither you nor your
fathers had known, to teach you that man
does not live on bread alone but on every
word that comes from the mouth of the
Lord.'

Deut 8: 2-3.

'Therefore I tell you, do not worry about your
life, what you will eat; or about your body,
what you will wear. Life is more than food,
and the body more than clothes.'

Luke 12: 22-23.

'Then Jesus declared, "I am the bread of
life. He who comes to me will never go
hungry, and he who believes in me will never
be thirsty.'

John 6: 35.

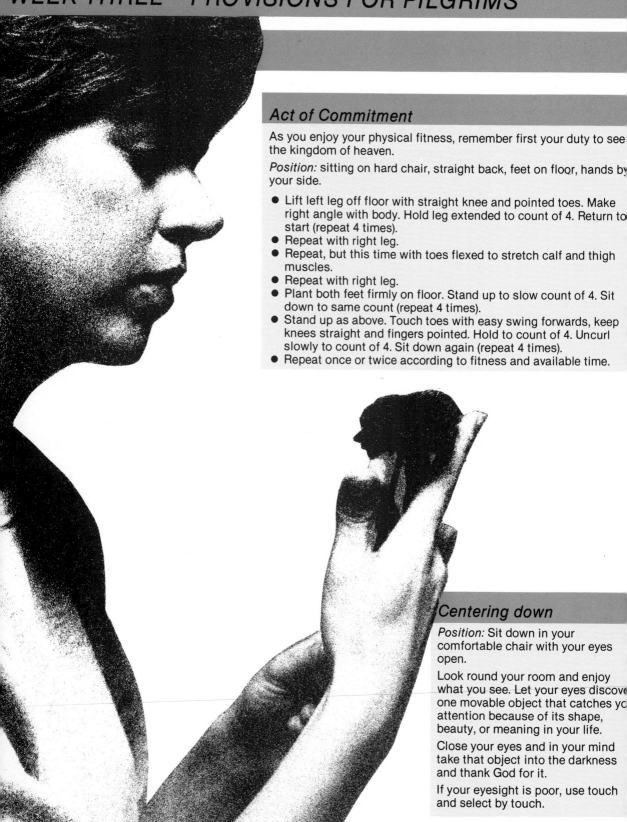

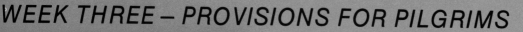

Act of Commitment

As you enjoy your physical fitness, remember first your duty to see the kingdom of heaven.

Position: sitting on hard chair, straight back, feet on floor, hands by your side.

- Lift left leg off floor with straight knee and pointed toes. Make right angle with body. Hold leg extended to count of 4. Return to start (repeat 4 times).
- Repeat with right leg.
- Repeat, but this time with toes flexed to stretch calf and thigh muscles.
- Repeat with right leg.
- Plant both feet firmly on floor. Stand up to slow count of 4. Sit down to same count (repeat 4 times).
- Stand up as above. Touch toes with easy swing forwards, keep knees straight and fingers pointed. Hold to count of 4. Uncurl slowly to count of 4. Sit down again (repeat 4 times).
- Repeat once or twice according to fitness and available time.

Centering down

Position: Sit down in your comfortable chair with your eyes open.

Look round your room and enjoy what you see. Let your eyes discover one movable object that catches your attention because of its shape, beauty, or meaning in your life.

Close your eyes and in your mind take that object into the darkness and thank God for it.

If your eyesight is poor, use touch and select by touch.

Prayer for a meeting

Slip to your knees. Keep your object in mind. Thank God for it, and for your ability to see it. At the same time, seek God who made it and you. *'O God, You are my God, earnestly I seek You.'* (Ps 63: 1.)

Meditation

Equipment: A jar of rice with a different seed; a small bowl.

Sit on the floor. Pour rice and seed into your bowl.

Shut your eyes: using only your fingers, find the seed. Then open your eyes to read:

> '"The kingdom of heaven is like treasure hidden in a field. When a man found it, he hid it again, and then in his joy went and sold all he had and bought that field.
>
> "Again, the kingdom of heaven is like a merchant looking for fine pearls. When he had found one of great value, he went away and sold everything he had and bought it."'
> (Matt 13: 44-46.)

Was it hard to find your seed in your rice bowl? How did you go about the task?

What does this mean in terms of your search for the kingdom of heaven?

Action for the day: hide your seed again. Find it again, this time with your eyes open.

Later reflection

Sit in your comfortable chair. Relax and center down. This time take your moveable object of beauty and feel it. Praise and thank God for it.

Did you see anything in a new way today? How did you seek the kingdom today?

God promises, 'Seek and you will find', so why not try to find that verse in Luke's gospel?

In your journal describe some ways in which you go about seeking for the kingdom of heaven here on earth.

Act of Commitment

As your body gets stronger each day, rejoice that Go
has helped you to keep going until nov

Position: lying flat on your back, hands by your sides
palms on floor, toes pointec

- Lift arms forwards and upwards over head to mee
on floor behind your head. Do this slowly to cour
of 4. Hold for 4 counts. Return arms to side to slov
count of 4, keeping stomach muscles tight (repeat
times

- Lift both legs off floor, knees bent, toes pointec
Curl up to your body in a tight ball. Use count c
4. Hold for 4. Straighten to 4 (repeat 4 times

- Pull stomach muscles tight. Repeat las
exercise, but keeping legs straight at knee
and making right angle, not bal

- Repeat second exercise at fast pace s
you lift buttocks off floor and swing leg
over your head to touch floor behind head
Keep abdominal muscles tight. If it's diff
cult, start with fists under your buttock:
Return to start (repeat 4 times

- Repeat last exercise with straight leg:
If you ca

- Sit up with straight legs, pushin
down slightly with hand:

Centering down

Position: sitting cross-legged on floor or cushion, hands on knees, palms upwards and slightly cupped.

Gather your thoughts and feelings into an attitude of expectant waiting. Once you have done that, you are ready.

Clear your mind of thoughts, but then allow whatever comes into it to stay with you.

If you feel totally blank say to yourself: *Come into my heart, Lord Jesus. Come.*

Prayer for a meeting

Continue to sit cross-legged. Wait expectantly. Lift up your hands in prayer: *'Give us this day our daily bread.'*

Meditation

Equipment: a cup of tea made in the cup with tea leaves and boiling water.

When cool, stir tea. Swallow a mouthful, leaves and all.

Put the cup down to let tea leaves settle. Read what Moses did when he found unpalatable water in the Desert of Shur:

'When they came to Marah, they could not drink its water because it was bitter. (That is why the place is called Marah.) So the people grumbled against Moses, saying, "What are we to drink?"

Then Moses cried out to the Lord, and the Lord showed him a piece of wood. He threw it into the water, and the water became sweet.' (Ex 15: 23-25a.)

Take another mouthful of tea. It should taste better.

God expects us to use intuition, knowledge and prayer together so that we can help God to help us.

Try to remember one occasion in your life where God helped you unexpectedly, but also helped you to help yourself.

Action for the day: enjoy the rest of your tea, or make a fresh cup.

Later reflection

Make yourself a drink. Sit down and enjoy it.

Thank God for helping you to help yourself.

Is there any way you could help people in the world whose water supply is polluted or scarce? Could that be part of God's answer to prayer?

In your journal list the names of organisations you know who are engaged in this kind of work. Choose one to support by prayer and gift in work or kind.

Act of Commitment

As you worship God with your body, reach out to receive God's gifts.

Position: kneeling, sitting on your heels, head high, hands at side.

- Tuck your chin on chest. Cross arms. Curl into ball; bend forwards to touch floor with forehead, to count of 4. Hold for 4 counts. Uncurl slowly to count of 4 (repeat 4 times).
- From starting position, kneel up slowly; at same time sweep extended arms forwards over your head, then outwards into sideways extension at shoulder level. Do this to count of 4. Hold cross-shaped position for 4 counts. Return hands to side and sit back on heels slowly to count of 4 (repeat 4 times).
- Repeat but rise into standing position as you sweep arms upwards over your head. At end, kneel.
- In starting position, extend arms sideways and up to count of 2. Clap hands above head twice; return to start (repeat 4 times).
- Repeat two or three times, according to available time.

Centering down

Position: sitting on the floor, legs curled up and slightly to one side, rather as if you were at a picnic.

Close your eyes. Relax, using breathing to help if you still need to do that.

Allow your mind to think about a previous occasion when you were sitting as you are sitting now. Enjoy the memory. Thank God for it.

Empty your mind now of all its images. Prepare for the unexpected as you dwel momentarily in darkness and silence.

Prayer for a meeting

God knows what we need before we ask; yet we are bidden by Jesus to ask. So ask God, quite simply and in your own words, to supply your needs today.

Sit comfortably on the floor in your 'picnic position'. Relax and let the tiredness drain out of you.

Think about today. Recall what you have been given today, by God, directly or through other people.

In your journal write about one gift you have been given today.

Meditation

Equipment: your two identically wrapped packages of nuts and raisins.

Place packages where you can easily reach them.

Close your eyes. Imagine yourself going out into the countryside to hear Jesus preach. The crowd is huge. You can't get very close to Jesus; and you can't hear him very well, but you get the gist of what he's saying. It's late. You've had no food. Suddenly, you're handed a gift of food, out of the blue. To your surprise everyone else is eating too. Later, you hear the full story of what happened when Jesus asked his disciples to feed the people:

'They said to him, "That would take eight months of a man's wages! Are we to go and spend that much on bread and give it to them to eat?"

"How many loaves do you have?" he asked. "Go and see."

When they had found out, they said, "Five – and two fish."' (Mark 6: 37-38.)

You know the rest.

What might you have felt if you'd unexpectedly received that gift of bread and fish?

When did God last give you a present? What was it?

Action for the day: thank God for all that you have been given and will be given. Choose one packet; open it and eat nuts or raisins with joy.

Act of Commitment

As you work at this exercise today remember that physical endurance is a kind of mirror of your capacity for spiritual endurance.

Position: standing upright, hands by your side. You'll need a timer for 4 minutes.

- Close your eyes. Collect your energy by taking 4 deep slow breaths; breathe in through nose, out through mouth.
- This is the only 'warm up' exercise today, and you've got to try to keep going for 4 minutes.

  Mark time on one spot, at first slowly, then quickly, then vary the pace to suit yourself, your mood and your muscles.

Some of you may find it easy to keep going for the whole time, others harder. If you have to give up, don't worry, just note the time you lasted so that you can compare your fitness now with later fitness.

If you know that you are very fit already, you can try this exercise out with a skipping rope, skipping continuously for the whole period of 4 minutes.

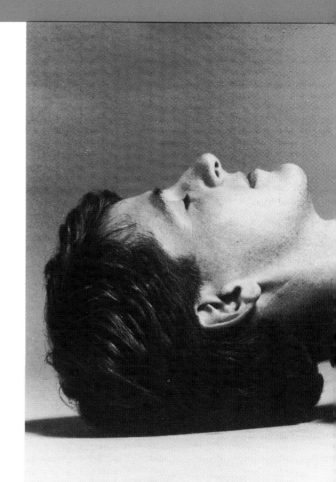

Centering down

Position: lying on the floor, on your back.

Let the ache ease out of your body. Enjoy the feel of the floor supporting your weight.

Close your eyes. Focus on your breathing. Slow and deepen it.

Enter the still silence. Use *love* as a word to steady your mind if you need to.

Prayer for a meeting

Kneel upright. Fold your hands in prayer. Praise God, *'Praise the Lord, O my soul'.*

Meditation

Equipment: box of matches, candle; needle and thread.

One gift we need for pilgrimage is the ability to persevere when the going gets rough. We can acquire this through enduring sufferings, mainly small ones.

Read aloud:

'God did not give us a spirit of timidity, but a spirit of power, of love and of self-discipline.

So do not be ashamed to testify about our Lord, or ashamed of me his prisoner. But join with me in suffering for the gospel, by the power of God, who has saved us and called us to a holy life – not because of anything we have done, but because of his own purpose and grace.' (2 Tim 1: 7-9.)

Endurance is often limited to purpose.

Take a match and needle. Lay them side by side. Try to break each in half.

Strike another match. Try to light your needle.

Are you more like a match in God's hands, or a needle? God needs both.

What small sufferings have helped you to learn to endure?

Action for the day: light the candle with your match; threat your needle.

Later reflection

Find your comfortable chair and relax in it.

Center down and thank God for your day.

Think about your meditation again. How can you best fulfil God's purposes? Could God want you to change?

In your journal write down one way in which you could become more like the person God wants you to be, and so fulfil the purpose you have been created for.

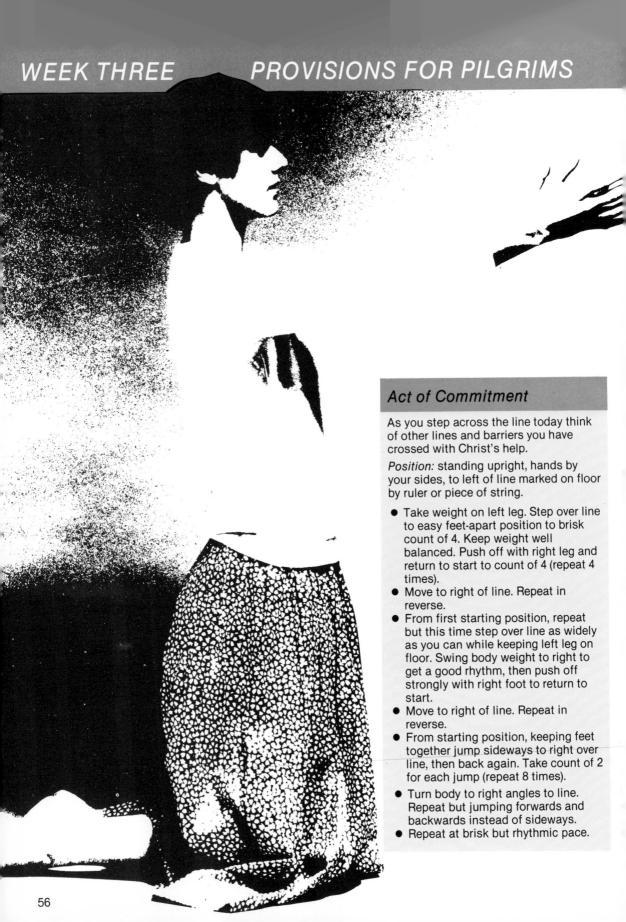

Act of Commitment

As you step across the line today think of other lines and barriers you have crossed with Christ's help.

Position: standing upright, hands by your sides, to left of line marked on floor by ruler or piece of string.

- Take weight on left leg. Step over line to easy feet-apart position to brisk count of 4. Keep weight well balanced. Push off with right leg and return to start to count of 4 (repeat 4 times).
- Move to right of line. Repeat in reverse.
- From first starting position, repeat but this time step over line as widely as you can while keeping left leg on floor. Swing body weight to right to get a good rhythm, then push off strongly with right foot to return to start.
- Move to right of line. Repeat in reverse.
- From starting position, keeping feet together jump sideways to right over line, then back again. Take count of 2 for each jump (repeat 8 times).
- Turn body to right angles to line. Repeat but jumping forwards and backwards instead of sideways.
- Repeat at brisk but rhythmic pace.

Centering down

Position: lying prone on floor, elbows bent, hands under forehead to support head.

Feel the floor under the weight of your body.

Allow your breathing to deepen and quieten. Be still and humble in your spirit as you adore God by prostrating your body.

If it is difficult to get your mind still say: *'Lord, I am not high minded: I have no proud looks.'*

Prayer for a meeting

Kneel upright with your arms outstretched to welcome Jesus, your friend and brother. Invite him into your heart: *'Come into my heart, Lord Jesus, there is room in my heart for You.'*

Meditation

Equipment: a pair of shoes, your bible.

If you go on a long journey you need a comfortable pair of shoes, well fitting, worn in, waterproof, snug, yet roomy.

Look at your shoes. Are they journey shoes? Have you provided yourself with the best spiritual 'shoes' for your Christian journey?

Read about Ruth's attitude towards her destiny when Naomi suggested they part company:

> 'But Ruth replied, "Don't urge me to leave you or to turn back from you. Where you go I will go, and where you stay I will stay. Your people will be my people and your God my God. Where you die I will die, and there I will be buried."' (Ruth 1: 16-17a.)

Do you have friendships like that?

Do you feel like Ruth did? Towards Jesus? Or others?

Action for the day: open your bible at Ephesians 6: 10-20 and read about the spiritual armour we need if we are to be Jesus' friends. Then put on your shoes.

Later reflection

Relax in your comfortable chair. Center down.

Take off your shoes. Thank God for your day. Choose one of your human friendships and think about your relationship. What makes it successful? What do you share with each other? How do your differences help each other?

In your journal describe that friend, and say how you think the friendship helps you to deepen your friendship with Jesus?

Act of Commitment

As you do your exercise, let your mind reach out to places in the world where people must travel many miles to fetch water from distant wells.

Position: mark a straight line on the floor (use string?) about 6 feet if possible. Stand at one end with a book at your feet; head up, stomach in, hands by your sides.

- Stand on tiptoes, then curtsey into deep knees bend. Pick up book. Place it on your head and stand up without holding on to book.
- Repeat 'knees bend' 4 times with book on head.
- With book still on head walk along your marked line and back again 4 times. (If you succeed in doing this without having to pick your book off the floor at least once, you should be trying this exercise with a glass of water instead of a book!)
- Put book aside. Walk along your marked line, putting one foot carefully in front of the other, keeping to the line without deviation. Return to start (repeat 4 times).
- From starting point hop length of line on one foot. Turn. Change feet and hop back on other foot (repeat 4 times).
- If you have time, repeat first three steps once.

Centering down

Position: standing upright with an easy, well balanced stance.

Close your eyes. Take 4 slow deep breaths, focussing your mind on the name of *Jesus*.

Step to the left. Repeat Jesus prayer and breathing, as before. Then return to start.

Step to the right and repeat. Then do the same but stepping forwards and then backwards in turn.

The Jesus prayer is your anchor wherever you have moved.

Prayer for a meeting

When your mind is stayed on Jesus you will be ready to pray: *'Fix my heart, O God, that I may move to do Your will.'*

Meditation

Equipment: a jug of oil; small bowl; towel to wipe hands.

Pour some oil into the bowl. Dip the fingers of one hand into the oil, then gently massage the palm of the other hand with oil until the skin feels soft.

Read part of the story of the man who was robbed and hurt, then left untended by the road to Jericho:

'But a Samaritan, as he travelled, came where the man was; and when he saw him, he took pity on him. He went to him and bandaged his wounds, pouring on oil and wine. Then he put the man on his own donkey, brought him to an inn and took care of him. The next day he took out two silver coins and gave them to the innkeeper. "Look after him," he said, "and when I return, I will reimburse you for any extra expense you may have."'
(Luke 10: 33-35.)

Have you known anyone who stopped his or her own journey to help you?

Have you ever done that for another person?

Remember those occasions. Pray for the people who helped you and whom you helped.

Is there anyone you know who needs your help today?

Action for the day: Put aside a sum of money equivalent to the sum you paid for the bottle of oil from which you filled your jug for the exercise. Let that be your Friday offering.

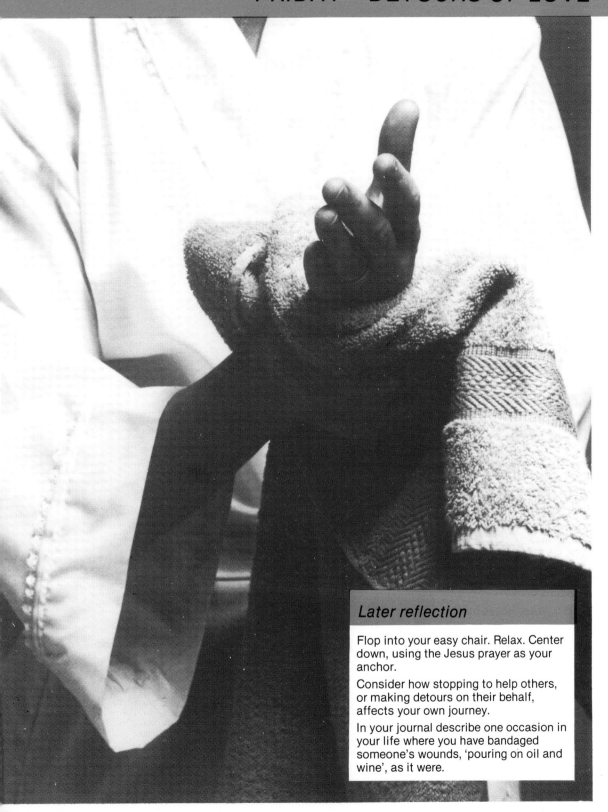

Later reflection

Flop into your easy chair. Relax. Center down, using the Jesus prayer as your anchor.

Consider how stopping to help others, or making detours on their behalf, affects your own journey.

In your journal describe one occasion in your life where you have bandaged someone's wounds, 'pouring on oil and wine', as it were.

Act of Commitment

Enjoy your physical exercises, but remember also to enjoy the rest that follows hard work.

Position: standing upright with tight stomach muscles, head held high and hands by your sides.

- Swing both arms vigorously in wide overhead circles until your arms begin to ache pleasantly. (Not less than 16 times.)
- Stand on left leg and kick right leg high, keeping knee straight and toes pointed. Repeat high kicks 16 times.
- Repeat standing on right leg, kicking with left.
- Holding both feet together, jump off floor. Continue to jump until your legs are moderately tired.
- Repeat until time is up.

(If you don't get in the least bit tired after 4 minutes of vigorous exercise, you're either very fit or not putting enough energy into the exercises.)

Centering down

Position: lying on the floor in the position of maximum rest, usually lying prone with head to one side and one leg slightly bent at knee, both arms flexed above head.

Immediately after 'warm up' get into position of maximum rest.

Sink deeply into this position of deep rest and swim into a state of deep relaxation. Enjoy it for at least two minutes.

Prayer for a meeting

Sit cross-legged, deeply relaxed. Center your mind on Jesus, your strength and stay. Remember his words: *'Come to me, all you who are weary and burdened, and I will give you rest.'* (Matt 11: 28).

Meditation

Equipment: a small pillow, a blanket, an alarm clock.

Imagine you have been on a long trek, like a day's march into the wilderness with the Israelites. In the evening you make camp. Later you lie down to sleep.

Use your pillow and blanket to find the most comfortable way of sleeping on the floor.

Rest is God given, and good. Read aloud the account in the bible telling us how the Iraelites knew when to rest:

'At the Lord's command the Israelites set out, and at his command they encamped. As long as the cloud stayed over the tabernacle, they remained in the camp...Whether by day or night, whenever the cloud lifted, they set out.' (Num 9: 18, 21b.)

That was 'living by faith', indeed. You and I usually use alarm clocks. All the time we rest at God's command and move at God's command.

Ask God to show you the meaning of rest in your own life and to guide you to its right use.

Action for the day: tomorrow is Sunday. Consider your needs. Set your alarm clock a little earlier or later than usual according to your understanding of God's will for you.

Later reflection

Flop into your chair and relax for about two minutes.

Did you take any rest during the day? Are you realistic about your need for rest and recreation? Have you got the balance between work, rest and play?

In your journal describe a memorable moment of rest which you really enjoyed and felt to be God given.

'Stand firm then, with the belt of truth buckled round your waist, with the breastplate of righteousness in place, and with your feet fitted with the readiness that comes from the gospel of peace. In addition to all this, take up the shield of faith, with which you can extinguish all the flaming arrows of the evil one. Take the helmet of salvation and the sword of the Spirit which is the word of God. And pray in the Spirit on all occasions with all kinds of prayers and requests. With this in mind, be alert and always keep on praying for all the saints.'

Eph 6: 14-18.

THE JOURNEY ITSELF

WEEK FOUR – GUIDELINES FOR LIVING

'Moses turned and went down the mountain
with the two tablets of the Testimony in his
hands. They were inscribed on both sides,
front and back. The tablets were the work of
God; the writing was the writing of God,
engraved on the tablets.'

Ex 32: 15-16.

'Set up roadsigns;
   put up guideposts.
Take note of the highway,
   the road that you take.'
         Jer 31: 21.

'Now when he saw the crowds, he went up
on a mountainside and sat down.

His disciples came to him, and he began to
teach them.'

Matt 5: 1-2.

Act of Commitment

As you stretch your body, let your mind reach for heaven.

Position: kneeling half back on your heels, body curled tightly into a ball, hands locking each arm, head well tucked in.

- Take 4 deep slow breaths before uncurling slowly to count of 4. Kneel upright; tuck toes under and try to stand up without using your hands. Stand to count of 4. Return to starting position slowly to 4 counts (repeat 4 times).

  (This is a difficult exercise. It will show you how fit you really are. Use your hands to push yourself off floor if you're not yet fit enough to do it.)

- Standing upright, extend arms with straight elbows sideways and overhead to touch above head. Do to count of 4. Hold for 4 counts. Return to sides to same count (repeat 4 times). Kneel.
- Repeat first exercise.
- From standing position, swing both arms forwards up and above head, jumping as high as you can while doing this, stretching upwards with pointed fingers (repeat 4 times).
- Repeat once more if time allows.

Centering down

Position: Curl yourself into a tight ball as if you were in your mother's womb.

Let the darkness enfold you. Let your imagination take you into the womb of your mother and then go beyond that to the moment of creation when God created heaven and earth.

Be still and wonder.

Prayer for a meeting

Uncurl from your centering position and sit back on your heels, ready to rise. Thank God for your life today; ask that it may be used to the glory of God.

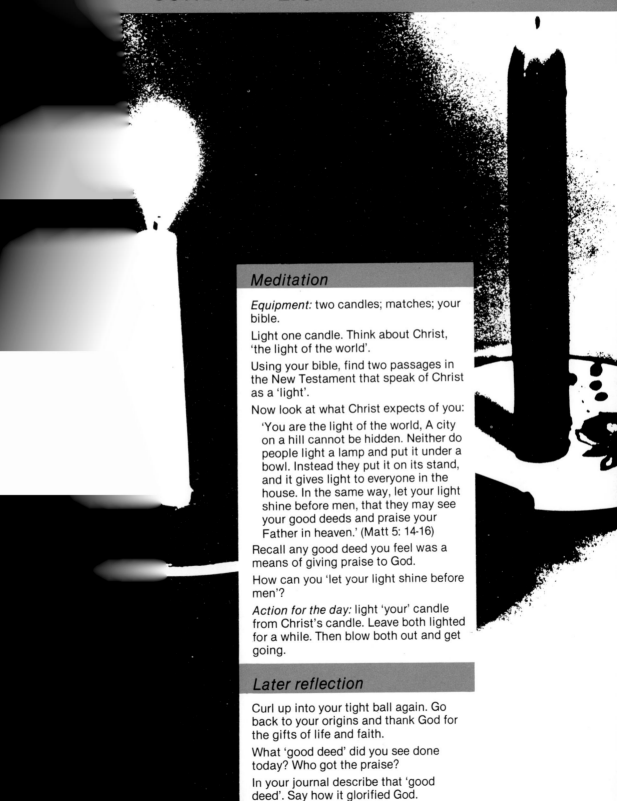

SUNDAY – LIGHTED LAMPS FOR GOD

Meditation

Equipment: two candles; matches; your bible.

Light one candle. Think about Christ, 'the light of the world'.

Using your bible, find two passages in the New Testament that speak of Christ as a 'light'.

Now look at what Christ expects of you:

'You are the light of the world, A city on a hill cannot be hidden. Neither do people light a lamp and put it under a bowl. Instead they put it on its stand, and it gives light to everyone in the house. In the same way, let your light shine before men, that they may see your good deeds and praise your Father in heaven.' (Matt 5: 14-16)

Recall any good deed you feel was a means of giving praise to God.

How can you 'let your light shine before men'?

Action for the day: light 'your' candle from Christ's candle. Leave both lighted for a while. Then blow both out and get going.

Later reflection

Curl up into your tight ball again. Go back to your origins and thank God for the gifts of life and faith.

What 'good deed' did you see done today? Who got the praise?

In your journal describe that 'good deed'. Say how it glorified God.

Act of Commitment

Learn to love the disciplines that set you free to do God's will.

Position: standing; legs slightly apart, hands by your side.

- Raise both arms sideways to shoulder level. Use count of 4. Then lean to left, flexing trunk; bring right arm overhead to try to touch left hand. 'Bounce' 4 times, to stretch and bend trunk. Return to start using same timing (repeat 4 times).
- Repeat bending to right and reaching with left arm.
- Raise arms sideways. Bend trunk forwards at hips to form right angle with floor. Do to count of 4, then 'bounce' forwards 4 times. Stand up slowly to count of 4 (repeat 4 times).
- Touch your toes to count of 4. Then sweep up into upright position, swinging arms forwards, upwards and into wide circle outwards as you stand. Use count of 4, then rest for 4 beats.
- Repeat 2 to 3 times, according to time available.

Centering down

Position: sitting on floor or cushion with bent up knees lightly clasped in hands.

Close your eyes. Breathe steadily and deeply. Watch the darkness. Plunge into it without fear for darkness is God's secret place.

Use *'Lord Jesus Christ, have mercy on me a sinner'* to help you if you find your darkness confusing or full of images.

Prayer for a meeting

Kneel upright and call to God: *'Out of the depths I cry to you, O Lord; O Lord, hear my voice.'* (Ps 130:1.)

Meditation

Equipment: a long piece of string; your bible.

Jesus has set us free from our sins; in our freedom we desire to serve God, so we willingly accept constraints on our freedoms. In the sermon on the mount Jesus spells this out as you can read:

'"Do not think that I have come to abolish the Law or the Prophets; I have not come to abolish them but to fulfil them...anyone who breaks one of the least of these commandments and teaches others to do the same will be called least in the kingdom of heaven, but whoever practises and teaches these commands will be called great in the kingdom of heaven."' (Matt 5: 17, 19.)

Take your piece of string and make 10 knots along it with spaces between. As you make each knot recall one of the 10 commandments. (Ex 20: 1-17.)

Which of them do you find most difficult to observe? Which sets you free from yourself?

What does freedom involve?

Action for the day: when you have made your knots, tie the ends of the string together; wear it round your neck today.

Later reflection

Curl up in your easy chair. Relax and center down.

Take your string necklace in your hands and feel the knots again. The commandments are guidelines for Christians. What other guidelines do you have?

In your journal describe one 'law' or guideline you feel to be important for you to keep because it sets you free and is a token of your committed love.

Meditation

Equipment: your notebook; pen or pencil.

In his sermon on the mount Jesus sets some difficult tasks for his disciples. One o these is to 'love your enemies'.

In your notebook write down the names of:

anyone who has hurt your feelings in the past month.

anyone who has exploited your good nature.

anyone who has failed to repay a loan.

anyone who has oppressed you or been an enemy to you.

If you can find no names to write, you are unusual. Then please do the exercise in reverse asking yourself whom you have hurt, exploited, used or oppressed.

Read aloud:

'"You have heard that it was said, 'Love your neighbour and hate your enemy.' But I tell you: Love your enemies and pray for those who persecute you, that you may be sons of your Father in heaven. He causes his sun to rise on the evil and the good, and sends rain on the righteous and the unrighteous."' (Matt 5: 43-45.)

Action for the day: shut your eyes and pray in turn for each of the names in your notebook.

Act of Commitment

As your hands work for God, let them plant the seeds of love that can overcome hatred and fear.

Position: standing upright, legs apart, hands by side.

- Bend forwards, leaning slightly to left. Reach forwards with right hand as if you were planting seeds and tap the floor in front of your feet in an arc from left to right 8 times. Stand up slowly (repeat 4 times).
- Repeat bending to right and reaching out with left hand.
- Repeat but this time plant only between your feet, moving backwards as you do so. Plant 8 seeds.
- From starting position swing right arm backwards and then overhead, as if you were chopping wood with an axe. 'Chop' near your left foot. Stand up (repeat 4 times).
- Repeat with left arm as your 'chopping' arm.
- Ease your back and rest.

Centering down

Position: start your meditative music; then lie prone with your head resting on your hands.

Enjoy your two to three minutes rest without anxiety or fussy thoughts.

If this is difficult use the phrase, *'Work is love made visible',* to help you to center yourself.

Prayer for a meeting

Curl yourself into a ball, with elbows on floor, knees tucked in under your body, head resting on cupped hands. In this way express your adoration of God without words.

Later reflection

Curl up into your tight ball.

Thank God for your day, for your friends and your enemies. Pray quietly and briefly for the people you thought about earlier in the day.

In your journal describe what it means to you to 'love your enemies' and to 'go two miles' when you are forced to go one.

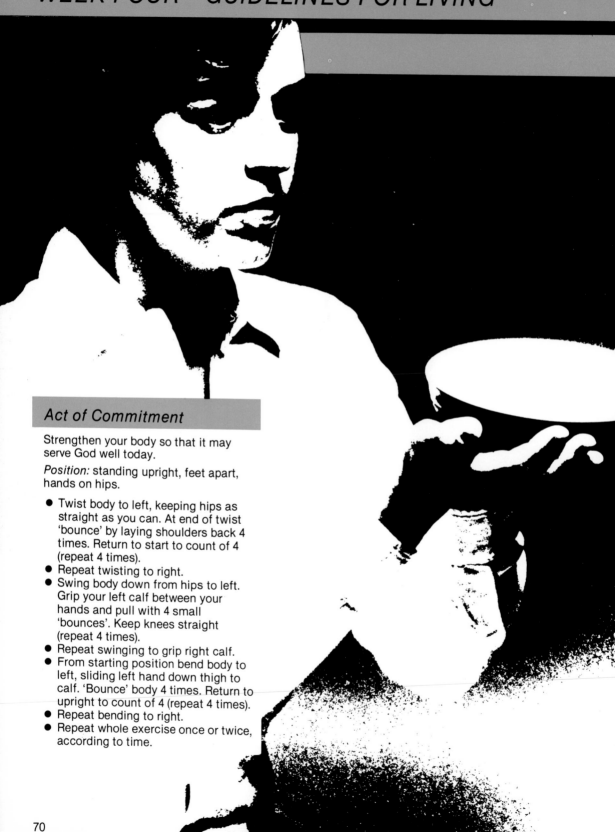

Act of Commitment

Strengthen your body so that it may serve God well today.

Position: standing upright, feet apart, hands on hips.

- Twist body to left, keeping hips as straight as you can. At end of twist 'bounce' by laying shoulders back 4 times. Return to start to count of 4 (repeat 4 times).
- Repeat twisting to right.
- Swing body down from hips to left. Grip your left calf between your hands and pull with 4 small 'bounces'. Keep knees straight (repeat 4 times).
- Repeat swinging to grip right calf.
- From starting position bend body to left, sliding left hand down thigh to calf. 'Bounce' body 4 times. Return to upright to count of 4 (repeat 4 times).
- Repeat bending to right.
- Repeat whole exercise once or twice, according to time.

Centering down

Position: sitting cross-legged on floor or cushion, with a bowl in your hands as if you were begging.

Feel the emptiness in that bowl and the emptiness in yourself needing to be filled with God's love.

Center your mind in your hands cupping the bowl. Right at the end of your centering allow yourself to think about a hungry child asking for food.

Prayer for a meeting

Still sitting with your hands cupped around your bowl, ask God for what you really need today, either spiritually or materially.

Meditation

Equipment: two small empty bowls; two coins of equal value.

Sit down in front of your empty bowls.

As a Christian you will be used to giving alms, but have you ever needed or received alms yourself?

Did the gift of alms make you feel happy or sad? Did you feel you needed to 'repay' the giver, or repay God if you did not know who your benefactor was?

Remember what Jesus said about almsgiving:

> '"But when you give to the needy, do not let your left hand know what your right hand is doing, so that your giving may be in secret. Then your Father who sees what is done in secret, will reward you."' (Matt 6: 3-4.)

How do you cope with that injunction? Is it enough to put money into the church plate?

Action for the day: put one coin into each bowl. Think how you might use one to give open pleasure to a friend, the other to give joy secretly to someone you know.

This is hard to do. You may not find an instant solution. Put each coin into separate compartments of your purse, or pockets.

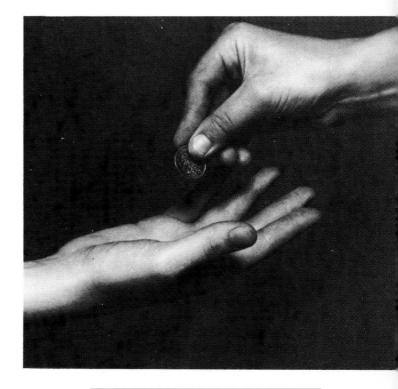

Later reflection

Flop into your easy chair and relax.

Thank God for the day. Recall its events, and your coins. How did you use your money? Or didn't you?

What other ways do you know of giving alms other than money?

In your journal write down all the ways you know of giving alms in secret to people you know without giving them an open gift of money.

Act of Commitment

As you teach your body to be flexible, ask God to mould and fit you for service.

Position: kneeling upright on the floor, hands by sides.

- Reach forwards into an 'all fours' position, keeping palms flat on floor. Rock yourself forwards and backwards using your arms as fulcrums. Use slow count and complete 8 swings forwards. Keep head and neck in line with spine.
- Keeping your hands on floor, raise buttocks, straighten knees, put feet flat on floor and 'walk' your feet as close to your hands as you can. Then push off from floor with hands and stand up.
- Lie down flat on back. Bring both knees up to chest. Grasp legs with both hands. Rock body and sit up (repeat 4 times).
- Lie down again. Keeping hands flat on floor by your side, raise both legs in air with straight knees. Bend sharply at hips, kick buttocks into air and bring both legs over your head to touch floor on far side if possible. Do this to count of 8. Return legs to starting position slowly to count of 8 (repeat 4 times).
- If you are not fit enough to do the last exercise or, perhaps, like me, are a little too old for it to be easy, put hands under buttocks, raise bottom and cycle for 8 complete revolutions with legs in air (repeat 4 times).

If there's any time left over, please rest.

Centering down

Position: find the most comfortable compact position for yourself and take it up. It is important to get comfortable ... use your easy chair if you feel like it.

Imagine yourself wrapped in a soft warm cloak on a cold night. Snuggle into its folds. Feel yourself enfolded by love as, indeed, you are by God's love. Dwell in it by faith.

Meditation

Equipment: seven stones; some kitchen foil; a plastic bag.

Set your stones in front of you. Prepare seven pieces of foil to wrap your stones in later on.

These stones represent the 7 continents of the world. Christians in all of them are united to each other by God through Christ. All use his prayer:

'Our Father in heaven,
hallowed be your name,
your kingdom come,
your will be done
on earth as it is in heaven.
Give us today our daily bread.
Forgive us our debts,
as we also have forgiven our debtors.
And lead us not into temptation,
but deliver us from the evil one.' (Matt 6: 9-13.)

Think about the needs of the people in each of the 8 continents. Symbolise the prayerful action of folding them in love by wrapping each stone separately in foil. Put them in bag to take with you.

Action for the day: at some stage of the day, unwrap each stone, praying for the people it represents as you do so. Replace stones together in bag.

ayer for a meeting

ll curled up, pray the Lord's prayer.

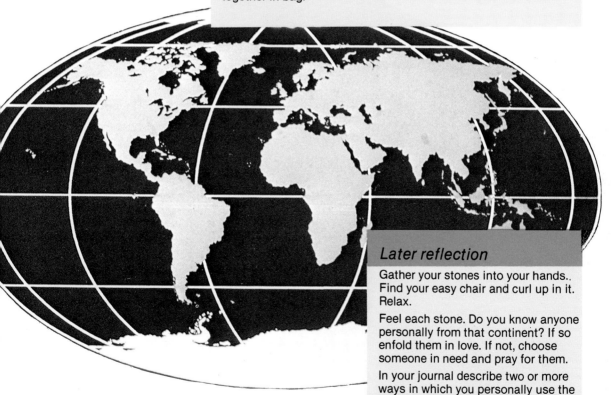

Later reflection

Gather your stones into your hands.. Find your easy chair and curl up in it. Relax.

Feel each stone. Do you know anyone personally from that continent? If so enfold them in love. If not, choose someone in need and pray for them.

In your journal describe two or more ways in which you personally use the Lord's prayer to deepen your spiritual life.

Act of Commitment

Take this opportunity to kick away some prejudices.

Position: standing upright, feet slightly apart, hands by sides.

- Take weight on left leg; kick with right as if you were kicking a ball forwards and to left (repeat 4 times).
- Repeat, kicking with left leg.
- Shift weight on to right leg; twist to right, get right arm ready to throw and then throw overhead as if hurling a javelin high and forwards. Follow through (repeat 4 times).
- Repeat throwing with left arm instead of right.
- Repeat but keep elbow close to body and with right arm throw upwards above head as if tossing a netball or basket ball into goal (repeat 4 times).
- Repeat using left arm to throw upwards.
- Repeat all exercises vigorously 2-3 times more according to time.

Centering down

Position: standing upright with your hands clasped just under chin, your head bowed.

Focus your mind on your breathing. Breathe in through your nose and out through your mouth so you can feel your warm breath on your hands.

Do this 4 times, then at end of a breath hold your breath for as long as is comfortable. Then take deep breath and settle into rhythmic breathing again.

Repeat until you find the still center of your being. Then whisper: '*Breathe on me breath of God*'.

Prayer for a meeting

Still standing, deepen your awareness of your dependence on God and your need of God's loving help in times of temptation and trial.

Later reflection

Curl into a tight ball, kneeling on the floor.

Center down and adore God. Thank Christ for taking your sins on himself. Pray to the Holy Spirit to lead you into all truth and teach you to forgive yourself as well as others.

In your journal copy out the first two verses of Matthew 7.

editation

quipment: a medium-sized bowl of ater and a towel; a sum of money uivalent to the cost of towel.

of us are capable of sin. We are en tempted to be critical of others, pecially when we see our faults in em, though it is hard for us to alise that, as Jesus knew so well:

'Why do you look at the speck of sawdust in your brother's eye and pay no attention to the plank in your own eye? How can you say to your brother, "Let me take the speck out of your eye," when all the time there is a plank in your own eye? You hypocrite, first take the plank out of your own eye, and then you will see clearly to remove the speck from your brother's eye.' (Matt 7: 3-5.)

hat sin do you often criticise when u see it in other people?

uld it be one of your own faults?

hat sin do you tolerate in other ople? Why?

hat sin do you need cleansing from w? Ask God to help you.

tion for the day: dip your finger in water and ask God to cleanse ch sense. Touch eyes, ears, nose, uth and hands. Dry your face and ds.

ve your money as usual.

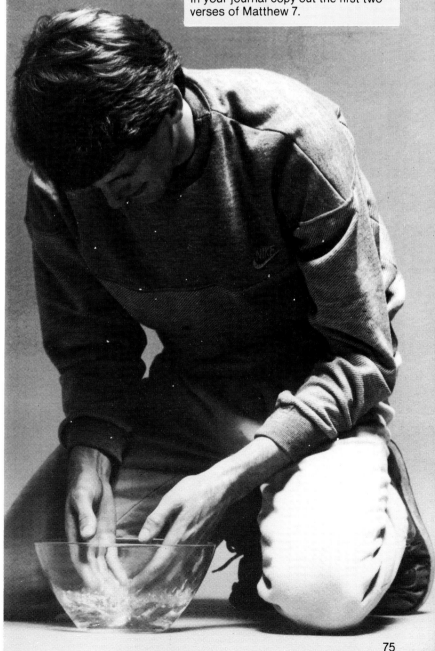

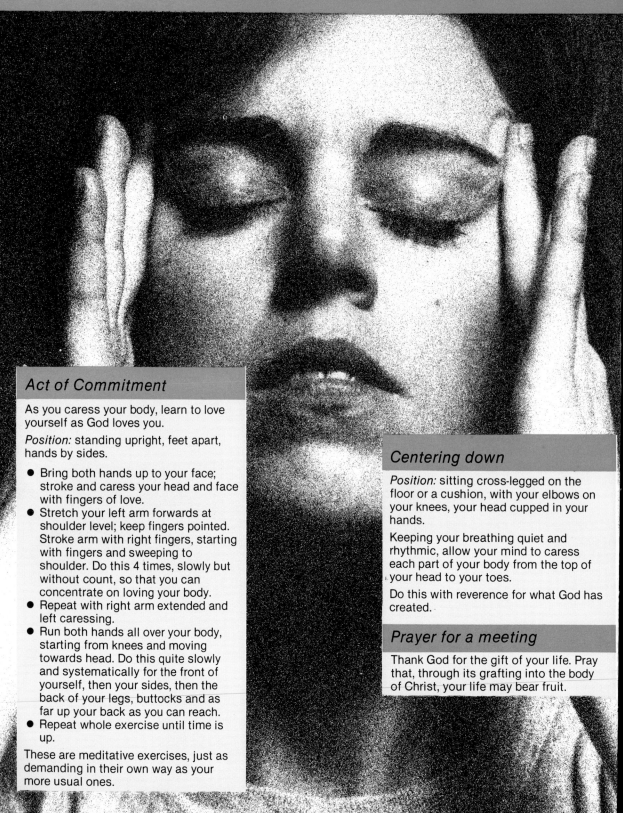

Act of Commitment

As you caress your body, learn to love yourself as God loves you.

Position: standing upright, feet apart, hands by sides.

- Bring both hands up to your face; stroke and caress your head and face with fingers of love.
- Stretch your left arm forwards at shoulder level; keep fingers pointed. Stroke arm with right fingers, starting with fingers and sweeping to shoulder. Do this 4 times, slowly but without count, so that you can concentrate on loving your body.
- Repeat with right arm extended and left caressing.
- Run both hands all over your body, starting from knees and moving towards head. Do this quite slowly and systematically for the front of yourself, then your sides, then the back of your legs, buttocks and as far up your back as you can reach.
- Repeat whole exercise until time is up.

These are meditative exercises, just as demanding in their own way as your more usual ones.

Centering down

Position: sitting cross-legged on the floor or a cushion, with your elbows on your knees, your head cupped in your hands.

Keeping your breathing quiet and rhythmic, allow your mind to caress each part of your body from the top of your head to your toes.

Do this with reverence for what God has created.

Prayer for a meeting

Thank God for the gift of your life. Pray that, through its grafting into the body of Christ, your life may bear fruit.

Meditation

Equipment: a twig from a bush or tree... or a picture of one.

Look at your twig. Consider its nature, its purpose, its relationship to the tree from which it came.

Consider your life as the branch of the true vine. How can you bear fruit? How will people know that your fruit is good?

Read aloud:

'"Watch out for false prophets. They come to you in sheep's clothing, but inwardly they are ferocious wolves. By their fruit you will recognise them. Do people pick grapes from thornbushes or figs from thistles? Likewise every good tree bears good fruit, but a bad tree bears bad fruit. A good tree cannot bear bad fruit, and a bad tree cannot bear good fruit. Every tree that does not bear good fruit is cut down and thrown into the fire. Thus, by their fruit you will recognise them."' (Matt 7: 15-20.)

Is it as easy as that? Fruit often looks good even when it is worm ridden inside. How can we know when the fruit and the tree are good?

Action for the day: put your twig into water. If you have time, read John 15: 1-17. If not, ask yourself how a gardener might go about helping that severed twig to become a new tree.

Later reflection

Get yourself comfortable in your easy chair. Relax and center down.

Go back to the grafting image... how do grafts take? How have you helped God to make sure that you are grafted properly into the life of Christ?

In your journal draw, or describe, grafting; the analogy helps but needs to be expanded in terms of our own life and faith, so try to put into words your own way of helping God to help you bear good fruit.

'"Blessed are the poor in spirit.
   for theirs is the kingdom of heaven.
Blessed are those who mourn,
   for they will be comforted.
Blessed are the meek,
   for they will inherit the earth.
Blessed are those who hunger and thirst for righteousness,
   for they will be filled.
Blessed are the merciful,
   for they will be shewn mercy.
Blessed are the pure in heart,
   for they will see God.
Blessed are the peacemakers,
   for they will be called sons of God.
Blessed are those who are persecuted because of righteousness,
   for theirs is the kingdom of heaven."'

                                        Matt 5: 3-10.

THE JOURNEY ITSELF

WEEK FIVE – TRAVELLING COMPANIONS

'He who walks with the wise grows
  wise,
  but a companion of fools suffers
  harm.'
Proverbs 13: 20.

'I am a friend to all who fear you,
  to all who follow your precepts.
The earth is filled with your love, O Lord;
  teach me your decrees.'
Ps 119: 63-4.

'Remember those earlier days after you had
received the light, when you stood your
ground in a great contest in the face of
suffering. Sometimes you were publically
exposed to insult and persecution; at other
times you stood side by side with those who
were so treated. You sympathised with
those in prison and joyfully accepted the
confiscation of your property, because you
knew that you yourselves had better and
lasting possessions. So do not throw away
your confidence; it will be richly rewarded.'
Heb 10: 32-35.

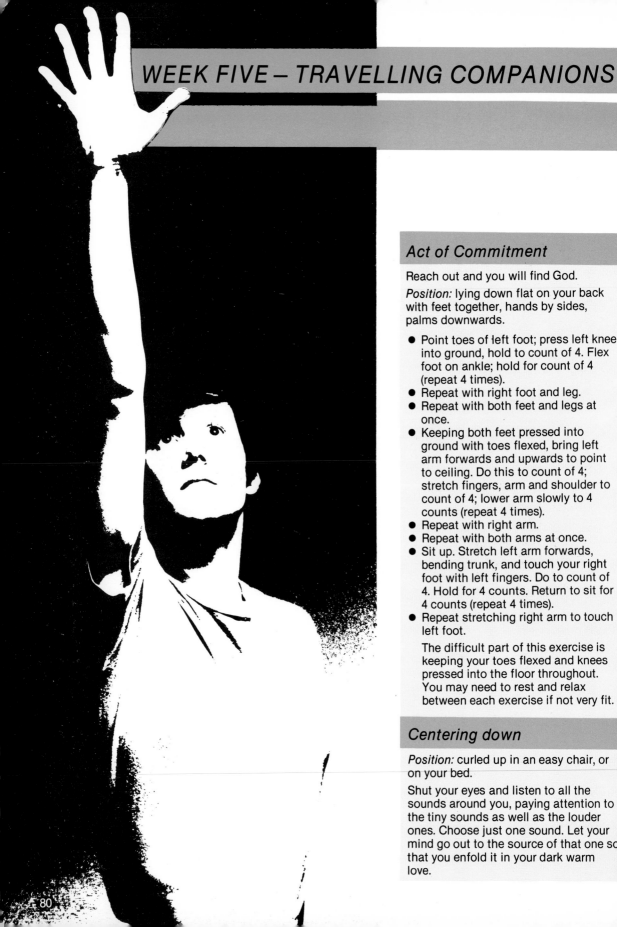

Act of Commitment

Reach out and you will find God.

Position: lying down flat on your back with feet together, hands by sides, palms downwards.

- Point toes of left foot; press left knee into ground, hold to count of 4. Flex foot on ankle; hold for count of 4 (repeat 4 times).
- Repeat with right foot and leg.
- Repeat with both feet and legs at once.
- Keeping both feet pressed into ground with toes flexed, bring left arm forwards and upwards to point to ceiling. Do this to count of 4; stretch fingers, arm and shoulder to count of 4; lower arm slowly to 4 counts (repeat 4 times).
- Repeat with right arm.
- Repeat with both arms at once.
- Sit up. Stretch left arm forwards, bending trunk, and touch your right foot with left fingers. Do to count of 4. Hold for 4 counts. Return to sit for 4 counts (repeat 4 times).
- Repeat stretching right arm to touch left foot.

  The difficult part of this exercise is keeping your toes flexed and knees pressed into the floor throughout. You may need to rest and relax between each exercise if not very fit.

Centering down

Position: curled up in an easy chair, or on your bed.

Shut your eyes and listen to all the sounds around you, paying attention to the tiny sounds as well as the louder ones. Choose just one sound. Let your mind go out to the source of that one so that you enfold it in your dark warm love.

Prayer for a meeting

Sit upright and alert in your chair. Reach out to God with your whole being: *'If I go up to the heavens, you are there; If I make my bed in the depths, you are there.'* (Ps 139:8.)

Meditation

Equipment: your bible; any picture of an angel.

The bible contains hundreds of references to angels. Just what do angels mean to you?

Look at your picture. Does it help?

Read aloud:

'In the year that King Uzziah died, I saw the Lord seated on a throne, high and exalted, and the train of his robe filled the temple. Above him were seraphs, each with six wings. With two wings they covered their faces, with two they covered their feet, and with two they were flying. And they were calling to one another:

"Holy, holy, holy is the Lord Almighty; the whole earth is full of his glory."' (Isa 6: 1-3.)

That's a wonderful vision of an almost undescribable reality.

What else do angels do in God's creation? What part did they play in Jesus' life? What part do they play in yours?

Action for the day: using Matthew's gospel remind yourself again of the part angels played in Jesus' life. You'll find references in chapters 1, 2, 4 and 28.

Later reflection

Get comfortable in your easy chair. Relax and center down, focussing on the sounds of this moment.

Using your bible, turn to the Acts of the Apostles and see the part played by angels in the life of the early Church. Look at chapters 1, 5, 8, 10, 12, 27.

Can you remember any time in your life when you met an angel?

In your journal describe your encounter, or say what angels mean to you.

Act of Commitment

As your body warms to its work, may your soul dance with love.

Position: standing upright, feet together, hands by side.

- Mark time, slowly at first, then quicker, finally ending in a 'running on the spot' time. Continue for about a minute.
- Stand still. Catch your breath. Then jump into feet-apart, feet-together (jumping jacks) rhythm. Repeat for 8 jumps.
- Standing on left leg, raise right leg sideways and jump, bringing left leg sideways to meet right in 'scissors'-like movement before returning to standing position. Repeat 8 times.
- Repeat using your right leg for 'take off' and your left as a leader.
- With legs straight and plenty of 'spring' jump into the air. Use your arms and elbows to gain as much height as possible and point your toes. Jump 8 times.
- Hopefully you'll now feel pleasantly warm. Gentle yourself down by doing 4 'deep knees bend' exercises before you finish your 'warm up' for today.

Centering down

Position: sitting cross-legged on floor or cushion.

Enjoy the warmth of your body. Put the fingers of one hand on your pulse at the wrist of the other and feel the blood coursing through your body, your heart keeping you alive at each moment.

Center your thoughts on God who sustains you in life.

Prayer for a meeting

Thank God for the universe, the world, its elements, your environment, your very existence: *'Praise be to God, now and forever'*.

Meditation

Equipment: some water in a bowl; candle and matches.

Dip your fingers in the water; spread its coolness on your cheeks, moisten your lips and tongue. Reflect on the value of water and its dangers in our world.

Read about the creator of all our elements:

'The breath of God produces ice,
   and the broad waters become frozen.
He loads the clouds with moisture;
   he scatters his lightning through them.
At his direction they swirl around
   over the face of the whole earth
   to do whatever he commands them.
He brings the clouds to punish men,
   or to water his earth and show his love.'

(Job 37: 10-13.)

God allows us to use the elements: yet we remain vulnerable to their power over us.

How do you use the symbols of fire and water in your prayer?

Action for the day: watch out for news stories about fire and water today. Take newspaper cuttings or make notes. Then use the stories for your intercessions.

Later reflection

Curl up in your easy chair with a long cool drink. Light your candle.

Pray while you sip your drink and look at your candle. Pray as the Spirit moves you.

In your journal describe two stories, one about water, one about fire, that specially moved you to prayer today.

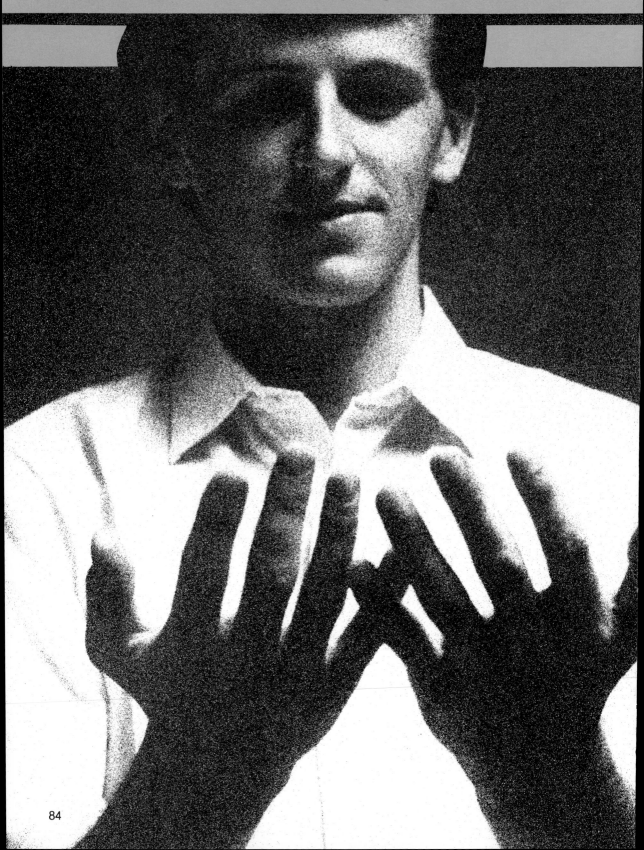

Act of Commitment

These exercises are meant to help you to realise the hard labour millions of people undertake in order to eat.

Position: standing upright, feet slightly apart, hands by your side.

- Rise on your toes, then sink into deep squat. Put both hands lightly on knees and rise to stand. Take 4 counts for squat, and 4 to rise (repeat 4 times).
- Repeat but this time only do 'knees bend' half way to squat to count of 2 and rise to count of 2. When upright, brace knees tight to count of 4 (repeat 4 times).
- Imagine you've got a spade in your hands. 'Dig' with your arms and hands, bending knees and spine to do so. Then 'lift' straightening knees and spine as you do so (repeat 4 times).
- Put your hands on your hips. Shrug and rotate your shoulders in clockwise direction for 8 circles.
- Repeat in reverse direction.
- Lift both arms into wide V above head to count of 4. Lean back and stretch to count of 4. Bring arms slowly to side to 4 counts (repeat 4 times).

(Repeat whole exercise once if you have time.)

Centering down

Position: sitting cross-legged on floor or cushion.

Put your hands together. Focus your mind on your fingers. Feel their sensitive tips; then use the tips of your fingers to feel your hair, your skin, your clothes, the floor covering.

Feel all that you feel with reverence for its being what it is.

Be still.

Prayer for a meeting

Thank God for the raw materials and creatures we have been given for our use. Ask God to help you to use them wisely and with respect.

Meditation

Equipment: a piece of ripe fruit; any edible raw vegetable; a few flowers, twigs and leaves in a small vase of water.

Look at all the things in front of you. How do they nourish you?

'Then God said, "I give you every seed-bearing plant on the face of the whole earth and every tree that has fruit with seed in it. They will be yours for food. And to all the beasts of the earth and all the birds of the air and all the creatures that move on the ground – everything that has the breath of life in it – I give every green plant for food." And it was so.'
(Gen 1: 29-30)

What is the difference between taking the life of a plant so that you may eat it to live and taking the life of an animal?

What does it mean to, 'eat simply in order that others may simply live'?

Action for the day: choose and eat the fruit or vegetable in front of you. Put the vase somewhere where it will nourish your eyes.

Later reflection

Curl up in your easy chair with your 'left over' food.
Relax...savour its goodness, thank God for it and eat it with pleasure.

Pray for those who are hungry at this moment.

In your journal note down the ways you have of trying to value and respect the foods you eat. Note also how you help to feed those who are hungry in our world.

Act of Commitment

Today, let the actions of your body be free to move your thoughts towards God as God wills.

Position: you will need a handy kilogram weight for these exercises. A kilogram bag of sugar, wrapped in a plastic bag, would do nicely. Sit cross-legged on the floor, weight on floor.

- Pick up weight with right hand, place it on outstretched left hand. Lift it to shoulder height to count of 4. Hold for 4 counts. Lower to floor level to 4 counts (repeat 4 times). Keep elbow straight, arm forwards.
- Repeat taking weight on right hand.
- Repeat but taking weight in both hands cupped.
- Put weight on left hand. Lift it close to body, as if you were about to throw a basket ball into goal ring. Raise arm high above head to count of 4. Hold for 4 counts. Return to start to 4 counts (repeat 4 times).
- Repeat with weight in right hand.
- Take weight in left hand. Raise arm sideways with straight elbow and bring weight overhead. Raise right arm to meet left. Transfer weight to right hand. Lower arm. Repeat in reverse direction (repeat 4 times).

(Some of you may have time to repeat the whole exercise once.)

Centering down

Position: kneeling, tucked into a ball with your head resting on your hands. Before settling, start tape of meditative music, timed to last at least 2 minutes.

Listen to the music. Give it your full attention. Allow your mind to be enfolded by it. Do not restrain your thoughts in any way today. Stay with any images and thoughts that come to you. God is in them somewhere, however odd they may seem.

Prayer for a meeting

Thank God for your ability to w
Ask God to help you to be awa
of the needs of animals who w
for you.

Meditation

Equipment: a picture of any large domestic animal used for food or work; eg: horse, cow, ox.

Look at your picture. Consider how your animal serves your needs.

What kind of resonsibility do we have towards animals we rear for food or work?

Read aloud:

'Six days do your work, but on the seventh day do not work, so that your ox and your donkey may rest and the slave born in your household, and the alien as well, may be refreshed. (Ex 23: 12.)

Times have changed many people's attitudes towards sabbath rest. What of our attitudes towards the animals we use for our good?

What do you think, or try to do, about organised cruelty towards animals which is carried out for the sake of human welfare or profit, such as vivisection, forced feeding, battery rearing?

Action for the day: note the names of each animal which has provided you with food and clothing today. If you are a vegan, note plants you have consumed. Pray for all who use or misuse those animals.

Later reflection

Relax in your easy chair. Center your thoughts on to the animals who have supplied your needs today. Consider ways of helping them.

In your journal write down the ways in which farming policies, nationally and internationally, affect the lives of other human beings and may affect the balance of nature. Describe your own attitudes to these policies. What might God be telling you to do in your own very small way?

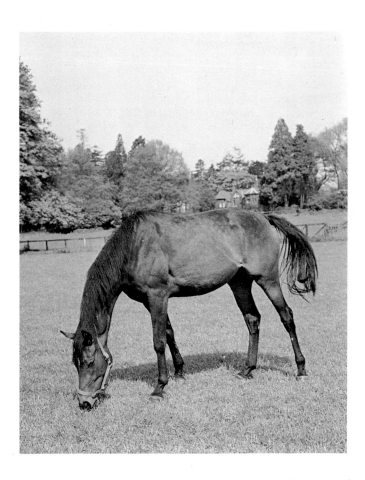

WEEK FIVE

TRAVELLING COMPANIONS

Act of Commitment

As you dance with grace, dance to glorify God with your body.

Position: standing upright, feet together, hands by side. Do exercises without music first time, with music second time.

- Imagine you are dancing to please an audience. Bring left arm across body to right hip level, then, keeping arms straight, fingers pointed, swing left arm up, over head, sideways and down again to left side to count of 8 (repeat 4 times).
- Repeat starting with right arm near left hip.
- Stretch left arm forwards taking weight on left leg. Stretch right arm and leg backwards, keeping all joints straight, to form an arabesque as dancers do. Use a slow count of 8. Return to stand (repeat 4 times).
- Repeat taking weight on right leg and leading with right arm forwards.
- Bring both arms forwards and upwards above head to form a graceful arc. At the same time stand on tiptoe and stretch your whole body upwards. Take 4 counts to rise, 4 to hold and 4 to return to stand (repeat 4 times).
- Repeat whole exercise to music.

Centering down

Position: any position where you can feel relaxed and yet alert. Arms need to be free.

Either play a short tape of meditative music, or make your own music, or hum or sing to yourself.

Let the music carry you: feel absorbed by it, yet absorbed also in God.

Prayer for a meeting

Thank God for all the creative skills that human beings have been able to use to bring spiritual nourishment to their fellow human beings.

Try singing your own prayer, using words or lilt.

Meditation

Equipment: any pictue or postcard that draws your eyes to its beauty; any short poem or prose which does the same.

Pick up your picture and poem/prose. Look at both long enough to choose the one that speaks to you most vividly today. Leave the other.

Look at your chosen work of art. Allow yourself to enjoy it for at least two minutes. (Use timer if necessary.)

Then read aloud, or sing:

'Praise the Lord...

Praise him with the sounding of the
                                    trumpet,
    praise him with the harp and lyre,
praise him with tambourine and
                                    dancing,
    praise him with the strings and
                                    flute,
praise him with the clash of cymbals,
    praise him with resounding
                                    cymbals.
Let everything that has breath,
    praise the Lord.'
                        (Ps 150: 1, 3-6.)

Which source of beauty is your habitual companion? How do you see beauty as part of your workshop?

Action for the day: pick up the poem or picture you didn't use in the meditation. Carry it with you and look at it sometime in the day.

Later reflection

Fetch your picture and poem. Curl up in your chair with them.

Relax and center down.

Enjoy both again.

In your journal make a note of the use you have made of the creative arts or beauty during this week of your life.

Act of Commitment

As you train your body to obey you today, remember that God can use you anywhere if you are willing and fit.

Position: lying prone, with forehead supported on your cupped hands.

- Keeping elbows bent, lift your head and shoulders off floor to count of 4. Hold for 4 counts. Lower head on to hands (repeat 4 times).
- Put hands by sides; roll from prone to supine position using shoulders and buttocks as sources of momentum. Roll back again (repeat 4 times).
- Repeat in opposite direction.
- Lying on your back, bend your knees, keep hands pressed against floor, raise your body off floor to rest on shoulders and feet. Count 4 to lift, 4 to hold, 4 to lower yourself (repeat 4 times).
- Lying on your back, bend knees up to chest. Grip legs with arms and rock to left, then to right in swift, large movements. Do 4 complete rocks.
- Lying on your back, catch your breath. Sit up without using your hands if you can, with a little push if you can't.

  (A few people may manage the whole exercise once more.)

Centering down

Position: sitting with legs outstretched in front of you, either on floor, or on bed if you prefer.

Feel your face and body with sensitive hands. Be tender and loving towards yourself as God is to you.

When you feel in tune with yourself, let your mind reach out to God. If you feel at sixes and sevens throughout the time, just accept that as your offering of time today.

Prayer for a meeting

Get ready for today's work by kneeling upright and offering your body to God for service to Christ in your brothers and sisters, whoever they are.

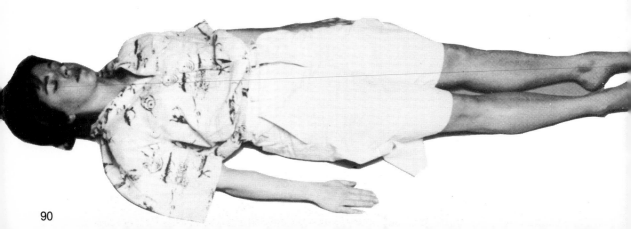

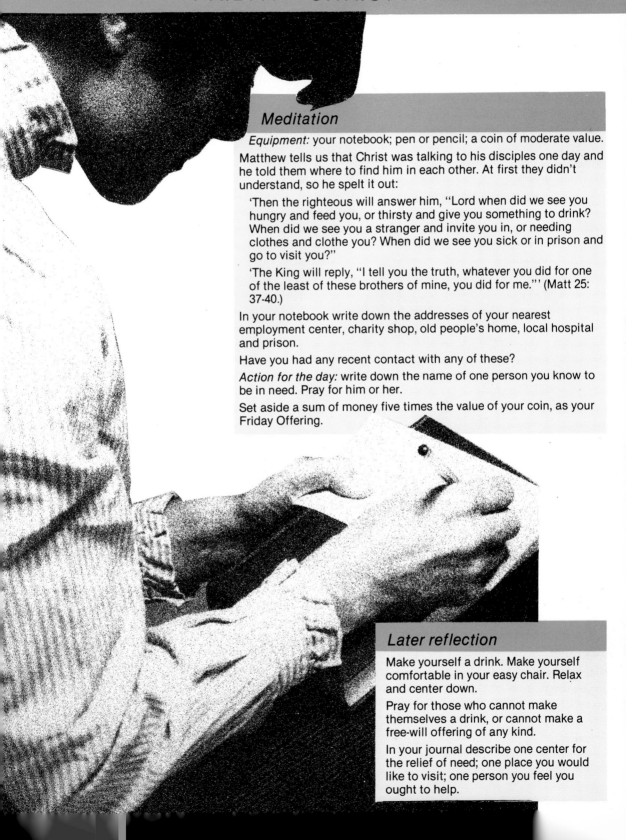

Meditation

Equipment: your notebook; pen or pencil; a coin of moderate value.

Matthew tells us that Christ was talking to his disciples one day and he told them where to find him in each other. At first they didn't understand, so he spelt it out:

'Then the righteous will answer him, "Lord when did we see you hungry and feed you, or thirsty and give you something to drink? When did we see you a stranger and invite you in, or needing clothes and clothe you? When did we see you sick or in prison and go to visit you?"

'The King will reply, "I tell you the truth, whatever you did for one of the least of these brothers of mine, you did for me."' (Matt 25: 37-40.)

In your notebook write down the addresses of your nearest employment center, charity shop, old people's home, local hospital and prison.

Have you had any recent contact with any of these?

Action for the day: write down the name of one person you know to be in need. Pray for him or her.

Set aside a sum of money five times the value of your coin, as your Friday Offering.

Later reflection

Make yourself a drink. Make yourself comfortable in your easy chair. Relax and center down.

Pray for those who cannot make themselves a drink, or cannot make a free-will offering of any kind.

In your journal describe one center for the relief of need; one place you would like to visit; one person you feel you ought to help.

Act of Commitment

Everything in creation has its own rhythm. Try to find your own deep rhythm as you allow your body to find this moment's rhythm.

Position: standing upright with feet together and hands by your side.

- Bring both hands in front of you, elbows bent, at waist level or just above, clap hands to 'Slow, quick quick, slow' rhythm. Return to side (repeat 4 times).
- Repeat clapping as above but this time clap overhead with extended arms.
- Repeat altering rhythm to slow steady handclap (4 claps).
- Repeat second step using rhythm of third.
- Put both hands on hips. Stamp out the rhythm of step one.
- Now have a time of free clapping, finding your own pace and rhythms, varying them as you feel.
- Stamp as you will, combining it with clapping if you feel like that. Continue until end of time.

Centering down

Position: sitting on floor cross-legged with hands resting on knees.

You are going to use a clapped rhythm to take you to prayer. This may seem strange at first, even wrong. Try to persevere; there's more to this than appears at first sight.

Clap: slow – quick – slow/slow – quick –
        Je   sus Christ, son   of
slow/slow – slow – slow.
God, I   love   you.

Repeat this rhythm clapping and let it carry your words into the depths of your being.

Prayer for a meeting

Change your position to kneel upright with your hands folded across your chest. Allow the stillness to enfold you as you wait for a meeting; that meeting always happens, though you may not be aware of it. Pray quietly: *'Jesus Christ, son of God, I love you.'*

Meditation

Equipment: your notebook; pen or pencil

Make 4 columns in your book, one each for winter/spring/summer/autumn. Under each heading write, almost at random, what each season is associated with in your own life. Then add the rhythms of festival and fast you associate with each season.

Read aloud:

'There is a time for everything, and a season for every activity under heaven:

a time to be born and a time to die,
a time to plant and a time to uproot,
a time to kill and a time to heal,
a time to tear down and a time to
                     build,
a time to weep and a time to laugh,
a time to mourn and a time to dance,'
                    (Eccles 3: 1-4.)

So it goes on. You can read the rest for yourself, later on.

Shut your eyes; ask God to show you how to use the natural rhythms in yourself, your environment, your church life to tune in to God's healing rhythms.

Action for the day: make a list of some of the events and seasons you find disturbing to harmony, and some you find helpful.

Later reflection

Lie on the floor or your bed. Relax completely. Center down using the natural rhythm of your breathing to help you.

Try to find ways in which your experience of good rhythms has or can overcome disruptive or disturbing rhythms, 'vibes' or 'atmospheres'.

In your journal make some suggestions for using your rhythms, times and seasons more creatively than you now do. If you're satisfied already, say why.

'If you have any encouragement from being united with Christ, if any comfort from his love, if any fellowship with the Spirit, if any tenderness and compassion, then make my joy complete by being like-minded, having the same love, being one in spirit and purpose. Do nothing out of selfish ambition or vain conceit, but in humility consider others better than yourselves. Each of you should look not only to your own interests, but also to the interests of others.'

Phil 2: 1-7.

THE JOURNEY ITSELF

WEEK SIX – MANNA IN THE DESERT

'But they soon forgot what he had done
   and did not wait for his counsel.
In the desert they gave in to their craving;
in the wasteland they put God to the test.'

Ps 106: 13-14.

'They did not thirst when he led them
   through the deserts;
he made water flow for them from the rock;
he split the rock
   and water gushed out.'

Isa 48: 21.

'Jesus, full of the Holy Spirit, returned from
the Jordan and was led by the Spirit in the
desert, where for forty days he was tempted
by the devil. He ate nothing during those days
and at the end of them he was hungry.'

Luke 4: 1-2.

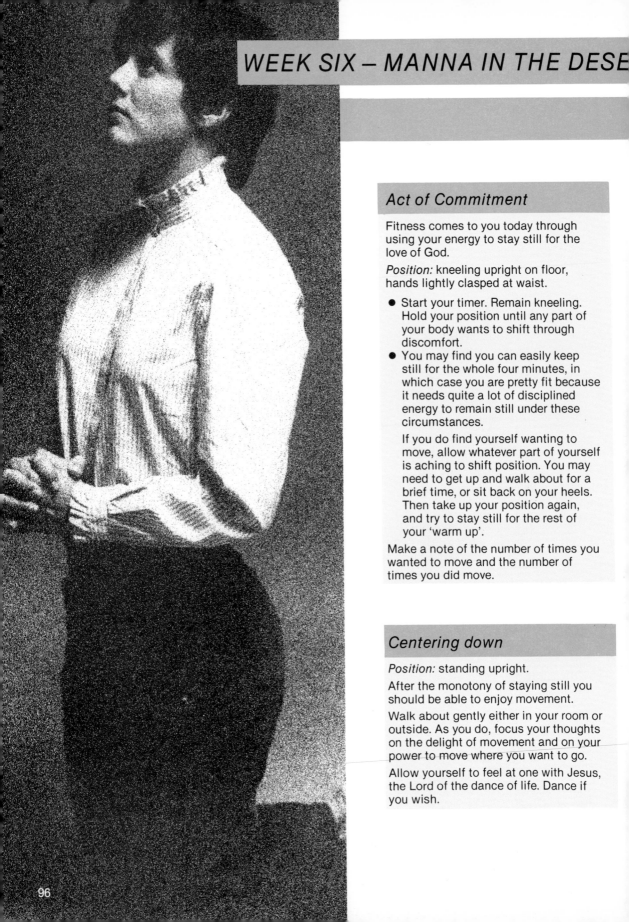

Act of Commitment

Fitness comes to you today through using your energy to stay still for the love of God.

Position: kneeling upright on floor, hands lightly clasped at waist.

- Start your timer. Remain kneeling. Hold your position until any part of your body wants to shift through discomfort.
- You may find you can easily keep still for the whole four minutes, in which case you are pretty fit because it needs quite a lot of disciplined energy to remain still under these circumstances.

  If you do find yourself wanting to move, allow whatever part of yourself is aching to shift position. You may need to get up and walk about for a brief time, or sit back on your heels. Then take up your position again, and try to stay still for the rest of your 'warm up'.

Make a note of the number of times you wanted to move and the number of times you did move.

Centering down

Position: standing upright.

After the monotony of staying still you should be able to enjoy movement.

Walk about gently either in your room or outside. As you do, focus your thoughts on the delight of movement and on your power to move where you want to go.

Allow yourself to feel at one with Jesus, the Lord of the dance of life. Dance if you wish.

Prayer for a meeting

Kneel again. Allow yourself to think about the people who cannot move freely because they are in prison, in refugee camps, housebound through illness or infirmity. Pray for anyone you know in that situation.

Meditation

Equipment: your bible; notebook; pen or pencil.

You've been on this journey several weeks. There comes a time for most people when the going gets tough. For Jesus it came when he was driven into the wilderness straight after the 'high' of his baptism:

> 'At once the Spirit sent him out into the desert, and he was in the desert for forty days, being tempted by Satan. He was with the wild animals, and angels attended him.'
> (Mark 1: 12-13.)

Jesus lived through that time of testing with the help of God's word. Have a look at Matthew 4: 1-11 if you need to remind yourself about it.

As a disciple of Jesus, you will be 'driven into the wilderness' too. Your temptations won't be the same ones as Jesus had to bear, but they will be testing.

How have you fared in the past?

What have you learned from aridity, monotony, hunger?

How are you preparing for next time?

Action for the day: write one or two favourite verses from the bible that you use when you need God's help in times of trial.

Later reflection

Sit cross-legged on the floor with your bible in your hands.

Relax and center down.

Recall your favourite verses that you use often. Try to find two more you could use for the future. (A concordance or cyclopedic index can be very helpful here.)

Pray for anyone in the wilderness.

In your journal write some of your special phrases.

Act of Commitment

As you let your burden drop today, think about Christ who bears the burden of your sins.

Position: standing upright with a hard backed book at your feet. Stand easy.

- Keeping back straight, squat down to pick book off floor. Stand up with it in your hands. Squat to return to floor (repeat 4 times).
- Squat. Put book on head. Rise to stand without holding on if possible. Remove book. Bend down to replace book on floor (repeat 4 times).
- Squat. Put book on head. Stand up. Walk up and down your room with book balanced. Take 100 paces. This may be a strain. If so, hold on to the book with one hand. Stop before 100 paces if your neck aches too much.
- Put your book down. Ease your neck, shoulders and back. Then lie down on the floor on your back and relax completely for the rest of the time. Enjoy that brief rest.

Centering down

Position: lying flat on your back on the floor.

Imagine you're lying on green grass on hot, sunny day, watching a balloon floating lazily in the sky, freed from constraints, blown about by soft currents of air.

Let your mind follow your imaginary balloon up and away. Feel the 'breath of God' urging your mind to freedom. Go beyond that thought to God whose will is your desire.

Prayer for a meeting

Sit up. Imagine yourself freed from the burden of sin. Humble yourself before God and ask for help. Listen for God's whisper of forgiveness, there even before you ask.

Meditation

Equipment: a heavy weight, like books or a sack of potatoes; a piece of paper; matches.

Carry your 'burden' across the room and back again. Let it represent a sin which is burdensome to you.

Read aloud:

'If we claim to be without sin, we deceive ourselves and the truth is not in us. If we confess our sins, he is faithful and just and will forgive us our sins and purify us from all unrighteousness. If we claim we have not sinned, we make him out to be a liar and his word has no place in our lives.' (1 John 1: 8-10.)

Thank God for your salvation. Ask for the gift of true repentence and conversion of life.

Have you a sin which is a burden to you? Offer it to God through Jesus Christ, 'the atoning sacrifice for our sins' (1 John 2: 2.)

Let God take that burden off you.

Action for the day: write your sin on your paper. It is a secret known only to God; writing it will make it a concrete admission. Burn the paper, allowing the sin to be burnt in the flame of God's love.

Later reflection

Lie on the floor on your back. Relax. Center down again.

Rejoice in your freedom. Thank God.

In your journal write a prayer of thankfulness to God for your salvation.

Act of Commitment

As you face today's challenge ask God to grant you the strength to meet tomorrow's temptations.

Position: standing upright, holding a ball which is suitable for bouncing.

- Bounce your ball, using both hands to catch and bounce it without moving your feet. Bounce 8 times, catching between each bounce.
- Using right hand only, bounce ball with patting movement, without catching between bounces. Bounce 8 times, without losing ball. Start again each time you lose control.
- Bounce ball with right hand. Catch it with left (repeat 4 times).
- Repeat in reverse direction.
- Now put the last two steps together, so that you are throwing ball from hand to hand via your bounce.

(Depending on how skilled you are, you can repeat the whole exercise several times. Hopefully, you'll gain skill each time as well as speed.)

Centering down

Position: kneeling on floor, sitting back on heels, arms folded across chest, back curled, head tucked in to rest on your knees or close to them.

This is not a comfortable position, nor it meant to be.

Allow yourself to be aware of discomfort. Keeping yourself still, let t discomfort become your center, then beyond.

It may be helpful to use the *Jesus* prayer to help you to center down through discomfort. This kind of exercise will train you to be able to pr under difficulties of other kinds.

Uncurl slowly at the end, lest you get dizzy.

Prayer for a meeting

Kneel upright. Gather into your mind all travellers especially today's refugees and any who are hungry, thirsty, anxious or exhausted. Say the Lord's Prayer for them.

Meditation

Equipment: a piece of bread; a glass of water; your bible.

You'll remember how God fed the weary, grumbling Israelites in the desert with water, manna and quails.

Thousands of years later Jesus fed thousands of hungry people with bread and fish. The next day he taught them about the meaning of what he had done:

'So they asked him, "What miraculous sign then will you give that we may see it and believe you? What will you do? Our forefathers ate the manna in the desert; as it is written: 'He gave them bread from heaven to eat.'"

Jesus said to them, "I tell you the truth, it is not Moses who has given you the bread from heaven, but it is my Father who gives you the true bread from heaven. For the bread of God is he who comes down from heaven and gives life to the world."' (John 6: 30-32.)

Many disciples found this and Jesus' subsequent teachings hard to accept: many 'turned back' and no longer followed him. (If you have time, read this passage now or later: all John 6.)

Have you been through a spiritual desert? Or known Christians who have endured exhaustion, aridity, apparent loss of faith? How did God send help to them?

Action for the day: even if you do not fully understand what you are doing eat and drink your bread and water.

Later reflection

Flop into your comfortable chair. Relax and center down.

Think about symbols and symbolic actions. How do they help or hinder your spiritual journey?

In your journal describe one time when you felt you were in a desert. How did God help then? Or not?

Act of Commitment

As you near the limits of your strength ask God to give you the humility to know when to stop.

Position: lying face down on the floor, head slightly left, turned to breathe comfortably, hands by sides.

- Roll on to right side, using head and shoulders to lead. Roll back (repeat 4 times).
- Roll right over on to back, then back again (repeat 4 times).
- Turn head to right. Repeat first step rolling to left.
- Repeat second step, rolling to left and over on to back.
- Lying prone, get into 'press up' position, and begin. Count the number of 'press ups' you can do before you begin to tire. Do two or, at most, three, more 'press ups' after you reach that point. Rest briefly.
- Roll onto your back. Sit up without using your arms to help you. Lie down and repeat 'sitting up' till you want to stop.

In this exercise you are invited to learn to know when to stop. Knowing your own limitations and limits is an important element in survival.

Centering down

Position: sitting in your comfortable chair.

Put your music on. Retire to your easy chair.

Relax and enjoy the easing of your body. Rest is also important if you are learning to survive hardships of any kind.

Enjoy the music and your rest without special effort. Remember to relax all your muscles as far as possible.

Prayer for a meeting

Sit up in an alert way. Pray for the wisdom to know when to push yourself and when to stop. *'Teach me to do Your will, for You are my God: may Your good spirit lead me on level ground.'* (Ps 143: 10.)

Meditation

Equipment: your notebook; pen or pencil. A large measure of humility.

Yes, I do mean humility. Yesterday you thought about spiritual deserts: today, think about material deserts like unemployment, divorce, bereavement or prolonged hardship of any kind.

Think back to the last time you were in that kind of desert, or knew someone who was going through one.

Who helped?

Read aloud:

> 'So, if you think you are standing firm, be careful that you don't fall! No temptation has seized you except what is common to man. And God is faithful: he will not let you be tempted beyond what you can bear. But when you are tempted, he will also provide a way out so that you can stand up under it.' (1 Cor 10: 12-13.)

It takes humility to acknowledge our vulnerability and to look for and accept God's 'way out'.

In your notebook write down any words or phrases from scripture you have found helpful in the past, and the names of people you can rely on for help.

Action for the day: write down the names of people you know who may be going through deserts now. Pray for them.

Later reflection

Sit in your comfortable chair. Put your legs up. Rest.

Thank God for your day, especially for anyone who helped you in any way today. Pray for those who need your help.

In your journal describe one material desert you have come through with God's help.

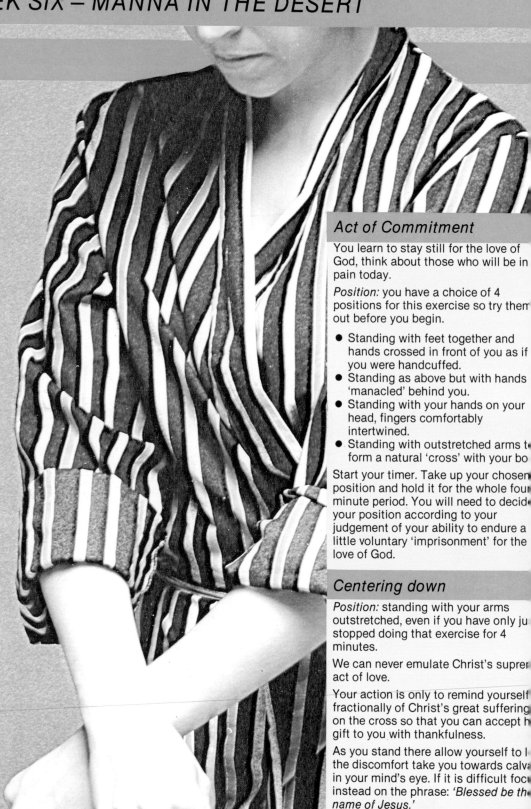

Act of Commitment

You learn to stay still for the love of God, think about those who will be in pain today.

Position: you have a choice of 4 positions for this exercise so try them out before you begin.

- Standing with feet together and hands crossed in front of you as if you were handcuffed.
- Standing as above but with hands 'manacled' behind you.
- Standing with your hands on your head, fingers comfortably intertwined.
- Standing with outstretched arms to form a natural 'cross' with your bo

Start your timer. Take up your chosen position and hold it for the whole four minute period. You will need to decide your position according to your judgement of your ability to endure a little voluntary 'imprisonment' for the love of God.

Centering down

Position: standing with your arms outstretched, even if you have only ju stopped doing that exercise for 4 minutes.

We can never emulate Christ's suprem act of love.

Your action is only to remind yourself fractionally of Christ's great suffering on the cross so that you can accept h gift to you with thankfulness.

As you stand there allow yourself to l the discomfort take you towards calva in your mind's eye. If it is difficult focu instead on the phrase: *'Blessed be th name of Jesus.'*

rayer for a meeting

eel in adoration and praise God. Then
k for God's gracious help: *'Hear my
y, O God; listen to my prayer.'*
s 61: 1.)

editation

uipment: a cross made by you out of
igs bound together or cardboard; your
tebook; pen or pencil.

old your cross. Let it symbolise the
ffering that comes to Christians
cause they follow Christ.

ad aloud:

Dear friends, do not be surprised at
the painful trial you are suffering, as
hough something strange were
happening to you. But rejoice that you
participate in the sufferings of Christ,
so that you may be overjoyed when
his glory is revealed. If you are
nsulted because of the name of
Christ, you are blessed, for the Spirit
of glory and of God rests on you.' (1
Peter 4: 12-14.)

s anything like that happened to you?

ut your eyes and recall it, even if it
emed a comparatively small witness.

ction for the day: write the names of
y Christians you know who have
ffered for Christ. Pray for them using
e Lord's prayer.

ater reflection

eel on the floor comfortably. Recall
e morning's exercise and center down.

s any suffering come your way today
cause of your faith? Rejoice if it has,
t rejoice, too, if you've been spared.

ay again for those who suffer today,
own or unknown.

your journal write about someone
u've known or heard about who
ffered for Christ. What happened?
ere they supported in their suffering?
w?

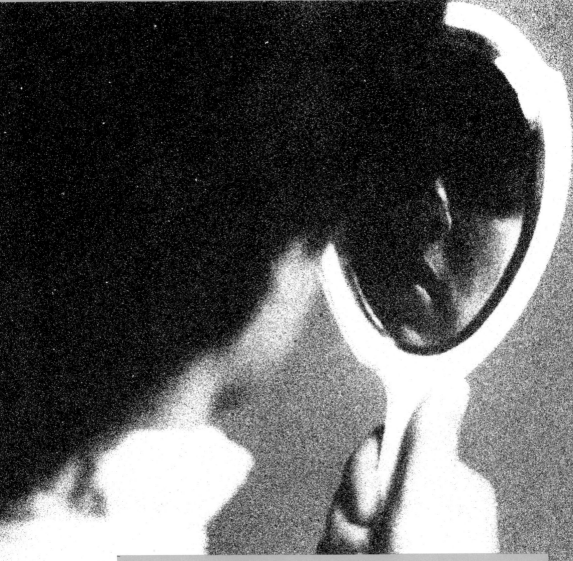

Act of Commitment

As you strengthen your legs for this day's journey, so strengthen your spirit to endure hardships along the way.

Position: lying on back, arms by your sides, palms pressed on floor.

- Bend your knees. Lift buttocks off ground on feet and shoulders. Hold to count of 4. Return to lying flat (repeat 4 times).
- Bend knees. Lift buttocks and body off floor to balance weight on shoulders. 'Cycle' your legs vigorously 8 times. Lower body and lie out flat (repeat 4 times). (If not too fit, put fisted hands under buttocks and 'cycle' legs like that.)
- If fit, push yourself into shoulder balance position but this time 'scissor' your legs, opening and shutting, 8 times. Return to start (repeat 4 times).
- Roll over on to front. Do 8 good 'press ups'.

(Rest if there's time left over.)

Centering down

Position: sitting cross-legged on floor.

Focus your mind on your breathing as it slows.

Then concentrate your thoughts on the air which supplies your body with the oxygen it needs for life. Try holding your breath at the beginning of each breath in, which will also be the end of each breath out. Do this for 4 breaths only.

Go back to normal breathing and be still.

You should be able to rejoice in your present fitness which will be better than it was, even if not yet as good as you would wish.

Prayer for a meeting

Let your mind turn outwards to those not so agile in body or mind as you. Pray for them wholeheartedly. '*Lord in your mercy, hear our prayer*'.

Meditation

Equipment: a mirror.

On every journey there are those who find the going easy: they stride out confidently and enjoy themselves. Others feel less fit; the journey is longer and harder than expected; they even despair of arriving.

Look at yourself in the mirror. What kind of a person do you see? Are you far ahead of the main group, or in it, or straggling?

Read aloud:

'We who are strong ought to bear with the failings of the weak and not to please ourselves. Each of us should please his neighbour for his good, to build him up.' (Rom 15: 1-2.)

How have you borne other people's failings this week?

If you feel you're a straggler, how have you acted towards those who are stronger and more competent than you?

Have you done anything this week to build up your neighbour?

Action for the day: count up the number of times you've been able to help someone this week; add in the number of times you've said a real thank you for help received. Multiply that sum by the value of the smallest coin in our currency. Set that aside as your gift to God this week.

Later reflection

Find your easy chair. Flop.
Think back over this day

Recall incidents today where you have given help, and received it. Thank God for today's blessings. In your journal describe one time in your life when you have been able to receive help from another person and you have seen the hand of God in that help.

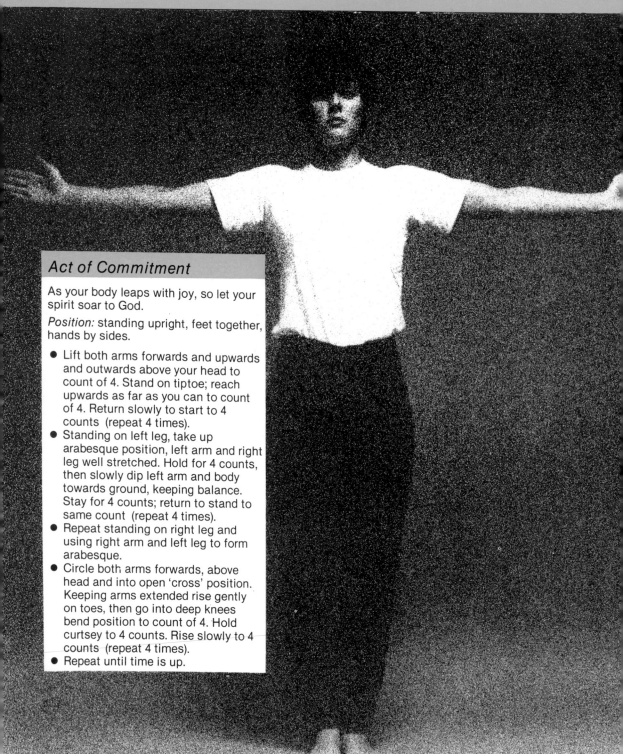

Act of Commitment

As your body leaps with joy, so let your spirit soar to God.

Position: standing upright, feet together, hands by sides.

- Lift both arms forwards and upwards and outwards above your head to count of 4. Stand on tiptoe; reach upwards as far as you can to count of 4. Return slowly to start to 4 counts (repeat 4 times).
- Standing on left leg, take up arabesque position, left arm and right leg well stretched. Hold for 4 counts, then slowly dip left arm and body towards ground, keeping balance. Stay for 4 counts; return to stand to same count (repeat 4 times).
- Repeat standing on right leg and using right arm and left leg to form arabesque.
- Circle both arms forwards, above head and into open 'cross' position. Keeping arms extended rise gently on toes, then go into deep knees bend position to count of 4. Hold curtsey to 4 counts. Rise slowly to 4 counts (repeat 4 times).
- Repeat until time is up.

Centering down

Position: sitting comfortably on floor as you please.

Imagine you have been on a desert journey. You reach your night halt at an oasis.

Allow yourself to relax into a feeling of relief and joy.

Still your mind with that kind of image. Do not worry if you slip beyond the image to the formless reality of encounter.

Prayer for a meeting

You have been walking in the desert this week. Thank God for the Holy Spirit's presence with you: *'Even though I walk through the valley of the shadow of death, I will fear no evil, for you are with me.'* (Ps 23: 4.)

Meditation

Equipment: a handful of sand in a bowl. (If you don't have sand, use salt as pretend sand.) Your notebook; pen or pencil.

Close your eyes. Run your fingers through the sand. Imagine it underfoot, blowing into your face, piled up in great soft drifts. Travelling in a desert taxes your strength.

Spiritual desert journeys can be just as arduous.

You will need hope if you are to endure and go on:

'We ourselves, who have the first fruits of the Spirit, groan inwardly as we wait eagerly for our adoption as sons, the redemption of our bodies. For in this hope we were saved. But hope that is seen is no hope at all. Who hopes for what he already has? But if we hope for what we do not yet have, we wait for it patiently.' (Rom 8: 23-26.)

How do you nourish the virtue of hope in your own life?

Action for the day: list some of the ways God provides for us to help us to hope for what we cannot see.

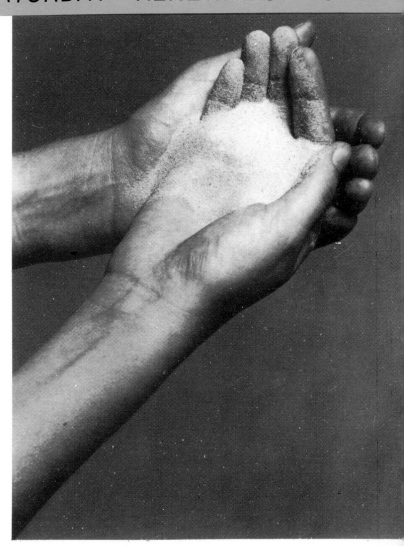

Later reflection

Curl up in your easy chair. Relax. Center down on that oasis, or your vision of your destination.

Use your bible to find and read some texts about hope. If you're not sure where to begin, have a look through Romans or Hebrews.

In your journal write down one of these texts that speak to you specially today. Try to learn it by heart.

'I consider that our present sufferings are not worth comparing with the glory that will be revealed in us. The creation waits in eager expectation for the sons of God to be revealed. For the creation was subjected to frustration, not by its own choice, but by the will of the one who subjected it, in hope that the creation itself will be liberated from its bondage to decay and brought into the glorious freedom of the children of God.'

Rom 8: 18-21.

THE JOURNEY ITSELF

WEEK SEVEN – LEAPS AND LANDINGS

'You, O Lord, keep my lamp burning;
  my God turns my darkness into light.
With your help I can advance against a troop;
  with my God I can scale a wall.'

Ps 18: 28-29.

Then will the eyes of the blind be opened
  and the ears of the deaf unstopped.
Then will the lame leap like a deer,
  and the mute tongue shout for joy.'

Isa 35: 5-6.

Blessed are you when men hate you,
  when they exclude you and insult you
and reject your name as evil,
  because of the Son of Man.

Rejoice in that day and leap for joy, because
great is your reward in heaven. For that is
how their fathers treated the prophets.'

Luke 6: 22-23.

Act of Commitment

As you strengthen your shoulders to carry God's burdens, ask God to give you a blessing for the tasks ahead.

Position: standing upright about one foot (30cms) away from a wall, hands by your sides.

- Lean back against the wall, taking your weight on your shoulders. Count 4, then put your head forward, push on your shoulders, lever yourself away from the wall to stand up. Count 4 (repeat 8 times).
- Stand further away from wall. Shrug your shoulders up and down vigorously 8 times. Rest for count of 4 (repeat 4 times).
- Now brace your shoulders back, hold for 4 counts, relax for 4 counts (repeat 4 times).
- Cross your arms in front of your chest. Grip arms with hands and hug tight. Hold for count of 4. Relax for 4 counts (repeat 4 times).
- Standing well away from wall, swing your arms in wide circles. Swing vigorously for 8 circles, rest for 4 counts (repeat 4 times).

SUNDAY – OLD MANTLES ON NEW SHOULDERS

Centering down

Position: kneeling on floor with your body resting on your heels, head and shoulders slightly bent forward as if to receive a garland of flowers.

Prepare to receive a blessing from God which could also be a yolk.

Focus your mind on your breathing. Deepen it into a slow steady rhythm, keeping the phrase, 'for my yoke is easy and my burden is light' going in your mind.

Find your still center of acceptance.

Prayer for a meeting

When you are ready to receive God's blessing and yoke, ask for that gift: *'I desire to do your will, O my God; your law is within my heart.'* (Ps 40: 8.)

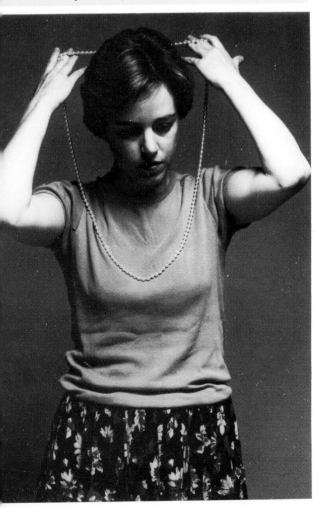

Meditation

Equipment: a long necklace, chain or scarf.

From time to time God's servants die, move on, or wish to pass their work on to younger shoulders.

Remember how Elijah's mantle fell on Elisha? When Elisha was left alone he knew he had inherited 'a double portion' of Elijah's spirit:

'He picked up the cloak that had fallen from Elijah and went back and stood on the bank of the Jordan. Then he took the cloak that had fallen from him and struck the water with it. "Where is now the Lord, the God of Elijah?" he asked. When he struck the water, it divided to the right and to the left, and he crossed over.' (2 Ki 2: 13-14.)

Would you be ready to pick up that mantle?

If you're already doing too much, should you be passing it on?

Is there any work in your church or community that needs doing and that you could do if your pride allowed you to ask?

Action for the day: think about that work, the mantle and the yoke. If you are ready, pick up your mantle (necklace etc) and put it on. Accept the burden or release it for other shoulders.

Later reflection

Curl up in your easy chair. Relax and center down.

Recall today's action. How do you feel about it now? Do you habitually shrink from offering to take on extra responsibility, or do you take on too much?

In your journal write out Matthew 11: 28-30. Describe what that means in your life.

Act of Commitment

As your body leaps with joy, so let your spirit soar to God.

Position: standing upright, feet together, hands by your sides. Choose somewhere where there's a bit of space, or go outside.

- Keeping feet together, leap into air and down again 8 times, in fast time.
- Repeat but this time intersperse each big jump with a little one, as if you were skipping. Complete 8 big jumps in all.
- Keeping feet together, leap forwards, then backwards to start: leap left, back to start; leap right, back to start; leap backwards, then forwards to start (repeat 4 times).
- Progress across room or space by a series of forward leaps, keeping feet together. Turn and leap back in the same way.
- Now bound across your space with long running strides. Put a real spring into your legs.
- Repeat whole exercise until your time is up.

Centering down

Position: sitting cross-legged on the floor, hands comfortably on your knees.

If you want to go places you'll get there most easily with long running strides. Use your memory to help you imagine yourself running easily along a country lane or across a sandy shore by the sea.

Let your mind run with you to meet God.

Whenever you come to an obstacle leap across it.

Prayer for a meeting

Thank God for the desire to run towards your goal. Ask God to help you to take a leap of faith whenever there are obstacles in the way or ditches to cross.

Meditation

Equipment: your bible.

In the past few weeks you've been asked to use many simple objects, and to do very ordinary tasks in your meditations. Sometimes you must have felt irritated or bewildered by the apparent naïvety of the exercise as Naaman did when Elisha told him to wash in the waters of Jordan:

'Naaman's servants went to him and said, "My father, if the prophet had told you to do some great thing, would you not have done it? How much more, then, when he tells you, 'Wash and be cleansed'?". So he went down and dipped himself in the Jordan seven times, as the man of God had told him, and his flesh was restored and became clean like that of a young boy.' (2 Ki 5: 13-14.)

Has anything like that ever happened to you? Could a small action of faith, like, for instance, going to a healing service, bring you great blessings unexpectedly?

Action for the day: using your bible, turn to the New Testament and find simple faith actions in the gospels that led to great blessings. Look for one or two according to time.

Later reflection

Curl up in your easy chair. Relax and center down.

Did you meet anyone today who expected too much and so couldn't receive God's blessing?

What blessings did you receive today?

In your journal recall one of the gospel stories you read today in your own words. What did it specially say to you about your own leaps and landings?

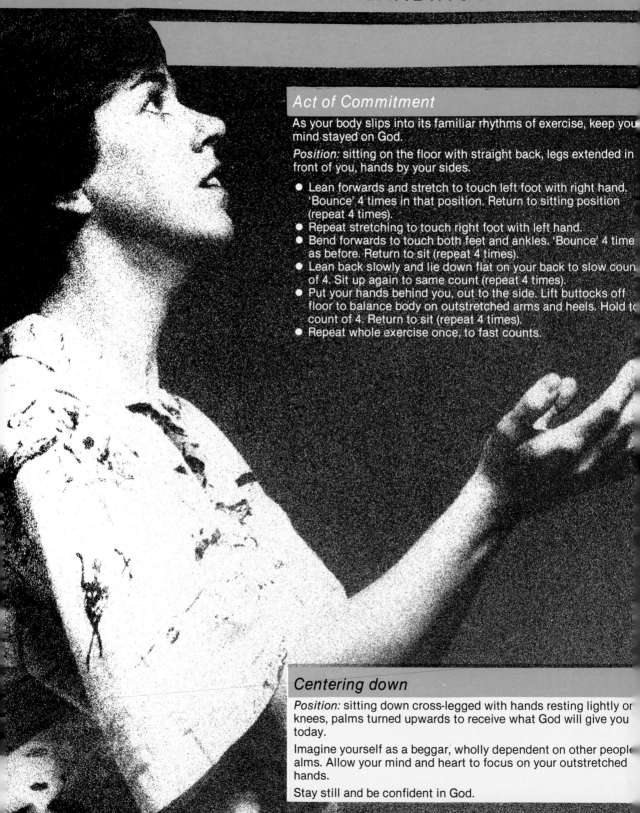

WEEK SEVEN – LEAPS AND LANDINGS

Act of Commitment

As your body slips into its familiar rhythms of exercise, keep you
mind stayed on God.

Position: sitting on the floor with straight back, legs extended in
front of you, hands by your sides.

- Lean forwards and stretch to touch left foot with right hand.
  'Bounce' 4 times in that position. Return to sitting position
  (repeat 4 times).
- Repeat stretching to touch right foot with left hand.
- Bend forwards to touch both feet and ankles. 'Bounce' 4 time
  as before. Return to sit (repeat 4 times).
- Lean back slowly and lie down flat on your back to slow coun
  of 4. Sit up again to same count (repeat 4 times).
- Put your hands behind you, out to the side. Lift buttocks off
  floor to balance body on outstretched arms and heels. Hold t
  count of 4. Return to sit (repeat 4 times).
- Repeat whole exercise once, to fast counts.

Centering down

Position: sitting down cross-legged with hands resting lightly or
knees, palms turned upwards to receive what God will give you
today.

Imagine yourself as a beggar, wholly dependent on other people
alms. Allow your mind and heart to focus on your outstretched
hands.

Stay still and be confident in God.

Prayer for a meeting

As a beggar before God you will know your need of alms. Close your eyes. Thank God for what you are given, knowing you will be given what you need for your salvation: *'May it be to me as you have said.'* (Luke 1: 38.)

Meditation

Equipment: a glass of water and an empty jug.

Pour half the water from the glass into the jug. Describe the glass and water to yourself.

Are you a natural optimist or a pessimist? Did you see that glass as half full or half empty? Try to be honest in your reply.

Our habitual responses condition us to expectations which may be false. Read aloud the story of what happened to some men brought to Elisha and his king after their capture. They expected to be killed:

'When the king of Israel saw them, he asked Elisha, "Shall I kill them, my father? Shall I kill them?"

"Do not kill them," he answered. "Would you kill men you have captured with your own sword or bow? Set food and water before them so that they may eat and drink and then go back to their master."' (2 Kings 6: 21-22.)

Those men received unexpected mercies. Later their masters made peace with Israel.

When did you last receive similar mercies?

Action for the day: consider what you want to do now with your glass, water and jug. Go and do it.

Later reflection

Relax in your easy chair. Recall the day's events.

Did anything unexpected happen to you today? Was it a source of blessing to you, or did you feel cursed?

Is there another way of thinking about the day that is different from the way you have just thought about it?

In your journal describe one incident where something you expected to happen didn't.

Act of Commitment

Today you face old problems and ne
challenges. Ask for God's help as yo
meet each difficulty.

Position: sitting on the floor, legs
extended forwards and slightly apart
hands by sides.

- Lean forward, place hands betwe
  legs and at same time move left l
  outwards sideways to widen spac
  between legs. Get it as far as you
  can; hold to count of 4. Return to
  straight (repeat 4 times).
- Repeat but keep left leg still and
  move right leg.
- Spread both legs; twist your body
  into an open 'splits' position if yo
  can. Do not force your joints. Jus
  observe what you can do. Try it,
  turning to right and then to left.
  Return to starting position.
- Bend knees; place feet firmly on
  floor, hands firmly on floor slight
  behind and to side of your body;
  off and rise to stand in one swift
  movement.

  (There's a knack to this; keep tryi
  till you succeed.)
- Raise arms sideways above head
  then dive to touch toes. Stand up
  swiftly (repeat 4 times).
- Place hands on hips. Do rapid 'kr
  bend', then stand up (repeat 8 tir

Centering down

Position: sitting on the floor in the r
comfortable position you have foun

You have been using new muscles
today as well as old ones. It may ta
minute or so to absorb what you ha
discovered, so focus your mind on
deep breathing, using the word *Goc*
still your mind.

Wait until you are really still and at
with your body before you begin to

Prayer for a meeting

Ask God to give you a new song to sing praise today. Lift your head and your hands as you pray.

Meditation

Equipment: two polythene bags, one old with a small hole in its bottom, one new, never used; half a glass of water, a medium-sized bowl; your bible.

Using your bowl to protect your floor, pour the water into one of the bags, then from that bag into the other.

There are several ways of doing this. Which way did you choose initially? Which way did you choose with experience?

Read aloud:

'And no-one pours new wine into old wine-skins. If he does the new wine will burst the skins, the wine will run out and the wine-skins will be ruined. No, new wine must be poured into new wine-skins.' (Luke 5: 37-38.)

What does this say to you in your personal life, work and church?

Even if you close your eyes and concentrate hard, this meditation may take longer than the allowed time. Don't hurry to finish, but allow God to give you more insights over the rest of the day.

Action for the day: open your bible and read the sting in the tail in our Lord's teaching in Luke 5: 39.

Later reflection

Flop in your easy chair; relax and center down.

Recall the morning's meditation exercise.

Did you find lots of different ways of tackling the problem? Did you find them all?

Can a leopard change its spots? Can you change your ways? If so, should you?

In your journal write about one new 'wine' that needed a new wine skin, some change that needed a whole new approach, new personnel, new structures if it was to succeed.

119

Act of Commitment

As you test your bodily fitness, so test your spiritual readiness to do God's will.

Position: lying on your left side on the floor, head, shoulders, buttocks in straight line; left arm under you, right arm by side.

- Raise right arm sideways and up to count of 4. Hold stretched for 4 counts. Return to side to same count (repeat 4 times).
- Keeping right arm by side, raise body on left elbow so that you're half lying, propped up. Hold for 4 counts. Lower body (repeat 4 times).
- Repeat but don't stop half way. Take weight on straightened arm and left foot so that you're doing sideways 'press up'. Hold position to count of 4. Lower body (repeat 4 times; use right arm as lever if you need to.)
- Roll over to right side and repeat using left arm as a lever and right arm as a counter-weight.
- Roll on to face down prone position. Do 4 half 'press ups' on bent elbows and 4 full straight arm 'press ups'.
- Roll on to your back. Relax.

Centering down

Position: lying flat on your back, fully relaxed, holding hands across your body.

Feel the support of the hard floor under you.

Close your eyes, deepen your breathing to a slow steady rhythm.

Drift into the darkness, holding your mind still and without thought for as long as you can. When you begin to think, say *'God, my God'*, and drift again.

Prayer for a meeting

As you pray to meet God pray too for the grace to discover your neighbour in that union with Christ. Pray the Lord's prayer in that unity.

Meditation

Equipment: candle, icon or holy picture; small statue if you have one; matches; your bible.

Light your candle; look at those images. Do you find them helpful in your worship? Are you tolerant about their use or 'non-use' in other people's traditions?

Remind yourself of how Jesus and Gentiles got together:

'Cornelius answered (Peter); "Four days ago I was in my house praying at this hour, at three in the afternoon. Suddenly a man in shining clothes stood before me and said, 'Cornelius, God has heard your prayer and remembered your gifts to the poor. Send to Joppa for Simon who is called Peter. He is a guest in the home of Simon the tanner, who lives by the sea.' So I sent for you immediately, and it was good of you to come. Now we are all here in the presence of God to listen to everything the Lord has commanded you to tell us."' (Acts 10: 30-33.)

Peter and Cornelius could overcome barriers, so why can't we? What does this story say about Christian unity without uniformity? (Read it all if you have time.)

Action for the day: return to your images. Pray for Christians who belong to two denominations other than yours.

Later reflection

Kneel today as a sign of penitence for Christian disunity. Center down, using the Jesus prayer.

Pray for someone you know who disagrees with you strongly, either within your own denomination or another. Stand with them in the body of Christ who presents you both to God, your creator.

In your journal describe what candles and images mean to you.

Act of Commitment

Let go, and let God take over.

Position: standing upright, feet together, holding a ball in both hands in front of you.

- Holding ball, lift both arms forwards to bring them overhead. Lean to left to count of 4. Hold for 4 counts. Return to straight for 4 counts. Lower arms (repeat 4 times).
- Repeat but lean to right.
- Raise ball above your head. Walk forwards and round the room as gracefully as you can. Enjoy the freedom of your feet.
- Put the ball between your feet. Repeat first step but do what you like with your arms once they are above your head, and you're leaning left.
- Repeat but lean to right.
- Try to walk forwards with your ball between your feet. Walk 4 steps; turn and return.
- Do what you please with your hands and feet until your four minutes is up.

Centering down

Position: sitting on the floor or cushion cross-legged with your ball held lightly in your hands on lap.

Allow your mind to focus on your hands. Deepen your breathing and slow it down. Accept the goodness of that ball and the limitations it places on your freedom.

Then put the ball down on the floor in front of you. Focus now on the freedom your hands have. Do what you feel moved by the Spirit to do.

Prayer for a meeting

Pray for grace to find your freedom in God's service. *'I will walk about in freedom, for I have sought out your precepts.'* (Ps 119: 45.)

Meditation

Equipment: your ball; the price of that ball in money.

Sit on the floor with the ball in your hands.

Doing that depends on your willingness to co-operate with my request.

Most of us can find freedom in obedience and service. Yet often we protest for seemingly good reasons.

When God asked Moses to speak as a prophet, Moses protested, for he said, 'I am slow of speech and tongue.'

'The Lord said to him, "Who gave man his mouth? Who makes him deaf or mute? Who gives him sight or makes him blind? Is it not I, the Lord? Now go: I will help you to speak and will teach you what to say."

But Moses said, "O Lord, please send someone else to do it."

Then the Lord's anger burned against Moses and he said, "What about your brother, Aaron the Levite? I know he can speak well...You shall speak to him and put words in his mouth; I will help both of you to speak and will teach you what to do."' (Ex 4: 11-14a; 15.)

How willing are you to accept God's call to service? Could you share it with others as Moses did?

Action for the day: set aside the price of your meditation ball as an offering for God.

Later reflection

Curl up in your chair. Relax.

Center down as you renew your offering of yourself for God's service.

Might God want you to serve in a particular way? Ought you to be sharing any special responsibility?

In your journal describe the 'pros' and 'cons' of shared responsibility.

Act of Commitment

Gather your energy to offer it all to (

Position: sitting on floor with straig
back; legs extended in front of you,
hands by your sides.

- Lean well forward; lock your han
  behind your head. Try to tuck you
  head on to your knees. Bounce
  forwards gently 4 times. Sit up
  (repeat 4 times).
- Sit upright; lock your hands behi
  your head; bounce your elbows b

in short jerks to tighten your sca
muscles. Bounce 4 times. Retur
sit (repeat 4 times).
- Lock your hands behind head. L
  down to slow count of 4; do this
  gently. Rest for 4 counts. Sit up
  to same count (repeat 4 times).
- Lie down again; roll from back t
  front into position ready to do e
  'press ups'. Raise yourself on el
  hold to count of 4. Lower yourse
  (repeat 4 times).
- Repeat but use full straight-arm
  'press ups'.

Centering down

Position: kneeling, sitting back on your heels; lock your fingers on your lap, palms touching your abdomen.

Focus your mind on your slow breathing but try to breathe with your abdominal muscles, allowing your hands to move up and down in a gentle rhythm.

Allow your mind to move with the rhythm, but if it is difficult to get still use the word *'God'* to help you.

Prayer for a meeting

Still kneeling lean forwards and reach out as if you wanted to touch the hem of Christ's robe as he passed by you. How wonderful that would be: *'To you, O Lord, I lift up my soul; in you I trust, O my God.'* (Ps 25: 1.)

Meditation

Equipment: yourself as you are today; your notebook; pen, pencil.

Have you ever longed to do something but been afraid to because you thought it silly or that others would misunderstand your action?

Do you remember the woman who had been ill for years and years and who found herself in a large crowd just as Jesus came by?

> 'When she heard about Jesus, she came up behind him in the crowd and touched his cloak, because she thought, "If I just touch his clothes, I will be healed." Immediately her bleeding stopped and she felt in her body that she was freed from her suffering.' (Mark 5: 27-29.)

Have you ever been in that sort of 'last chance' situation where you were willing to try to find help, even if you did make a fool of yourself?

Action for the day: in your notebook make a note of any occasion when you: (a) stood up in a crowd to ask a question? (b) made yourself conspicuous in Church? (c) asked for the 'laying on of hands' at a healing service in church?

Later reflection

Curl up in your easy chair. Relax and center down.

Look at today's page in your notebook. Is there anything in it for to-day? If not, why not? (There may be good reasons.)

If you have written today, recall the circumstances. What did you learn from the experience?

In your journal describe any occasion when you saw someone else making a fool of himself or herself for Christ's sake.

'Whatever happens, conduct yourselves in a manner worthy of the gospel of Christ. Then, whether I come and see you or only hear about you in my absence, I will know that you stand firm in one spirit, contending as one man for the faith of the gospel without being frightened in any way by those who oppose you. This is a sign to them that they will be destroyed, but that you will be saved — and that by God. For it has been granted to you on behalf of Christ not only to believe in him, but also to suffer for him, since you are going through the same struggle you saw I had, and how hear that I still have.'

Phil: 1: 27-30.

THE JOURNEY ITSELF

WEEK EIGHT – NEW HORIZONS

'Behold, I will create
new heavens and a new earth.
The former things will not be remembered,
nor will they come to mind.
But be glad and rejoice for ever
in what I will create.'

Isa 65: 17-18a.

'I will give them an undivided heart and put
a new spirit in them; I will remove from them
their heart of stone and give them a heart of
flesh. Then they will follow my decrees and
be careful to keep my laws. They will be my
people, and I will be their God.'

Ezek 11: 19-20.

'"A new command I give you: Love one
another. As I have loved you, so you must
love one another. By this all men will know
that you are my disciples, if you love one
another."'

John 13: 34-35.

Act of Commitment

As you learn to persevere, so ask God to build you into the person you are to become by God's grace.

Position: standing upright, feet slightly apart, hands by your sides.

- Keeping knees straight, lean forwards, extending both arms backwards and sideways. Then swing arms forwards in front of you and 'scissor' them 8 times. Stand up (repeat 4 times).
- Relax but this time 'scissor' arms behind you.

- Stand up straight. Raise your arms high above your head. Keeping elbows as straight as possible 'scissor' 8 times. Return to start (repeat 4 times).
- Lower your arms. Stand quite still while you take 4 deep slow breaths.
- Jump with feet apart, feet together rhythm for 8 complete jumps.
- Repeat vigorously if time allows.

Centering down

Position: sitting cross-legged on the floor with your hands in your lap.

Enjoy the warmth of your body and feel the blood coursing through it.

Shut your eyes and allow yourself to dwell in the welcome darkness.

Wait on God with hope.

If it is difficult to be still, center on the Lord's prayer, reciting it slowly to banish agitation.

Prayer for a meeting

Once you are centered in hope you are ready to receive god: *'You are my refuge and my shield. I have put my hope in your word.'* (Ps 119: 114.)

Meditation

Equipment: plasticine or other modelling material.

During the first week of this journey you made something new out of 'clay'. Since then you may have changed.

Use your 'clay' to create a 'new creature in Christ'. Then read aloud:

'Therefore, if anyone is in Christ, he is a new creation; the old has gone, the new has come! All this is from God, who reconciled us to himself through Christ and gave us the ministry of reconciliation: that God was reconciling the world to himself in Christ, not counting men's sins against them. And he has committed to us the message of reconciliation. We are therefore Christ's ambassadors, as though God were making his appeal through us.' (2 Cor 5: 17-20a.)

How does your 'clay' model express this?

Do you need to reshape it? Has the journey you have been on reshaped you in any way? How?

Action for the day: Leave your piece of work somewhere safe where you can look at it later on to see what it tells you.

Later reflection

Fetch your model. Get comfortable in your own way.

Center down by shutting your eyes and enclosing yourself in the warm friendly darkness you find there.

Open your eyes. Look at your model. Is it saying what you wanted it to say? If not, change it. If so, consider the meaning in your life of your becoming a 'new creation in Christ.'

In your journal, describe any changes you feel may have happened during the past few weeks.

WEEK EIGHT – NEW HORIZONS

Act of Commitment

Ask God to strengthen your legs so that you may follow Christ everywhere.

Position: lying flat on back, legs straight, head resting on hands, elbows bent.

- Lift both legs to form right angle with body. Raise head and shoulders; bring arms forward to clasp legs. Hold for 4 counts. Return to starting position. Rest for 4 counts (repeat 4 times).
- Keeping stomach muscles tight, lift legs as above. Cross and uncross legs in 'scissors' movement 4 times. Return legs to floor. Rest for 4 counts (repeat 4 times).
- Raise body on elbows with palms of hands pressed flat on floor. Lift legs as far as you can and 'scissor' them as above. (You may not yet be fit enough for this exercise but try it all the same.)
- From starting position, keeping legs on floor, sit up to count of 4. Rest for 4 counts. Lie down to same rhythm. Keep hands behind head throughout, and remember to tighten your abdominal muscles (repeat 4 times).

Centering down

Position: sitting comfortably on the floor. Try having one foot tucked under the opposite buttock and the other leg extended forwards. By now this should be easy, but if not, get into cross-legged position.

Close your eyes; picture an oasis in the desert.

Settle yourself by the water under a tree and wait.

Keep the image vivid and recall it to mind if your thoughts start wandering away.

Prayer for a meeting

Imagine Jesus coming towards you as you rest by the water. Kneel and worship him.

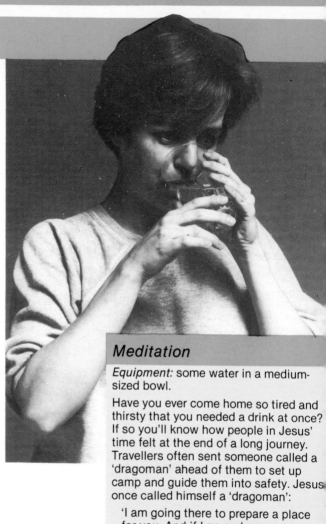

Meditation

Equipment: some water in a medium-sized bowl.

Have you ever come home so tired and thirsty that you needed a drink at once? If so you'll know how people in Jesus' time felt at the end of a long journey. Travellers often sent someone called a 'dragoman' ahead of them to set up camp and guide them into safety. Jesus once called himself a 'dragoman':

> 'I am going there to prepare a place for you. And if I go and prepare a place for you, I will come back and take you to be with me that you also may be where I am. You know the way to the place where I am going.' (John 14: 2b-4.)

Can you remember any resting places in your life where you have received a blessing from God?

If not, why not, seeing that Jesus goes on ahead and also comes back to escort you to your next resting place on the journey towards heaven?

Why haven't you been able to recognise him?

Action for the day: dip your hands into the cool water and refresh your face and hands. Drink a little of it out of cupped hands, sparingly as in a desert.

MONDAY – TRAVELLING WITH JESUS

Later reflection

Get yourself a long cool drink of water. Relax in your easy chair and center down.

Remember in prayer all who are thirsty every day for lack of water, or those who have to journey long distances to get it.

Remember those who are thirsty because they are ill and cannot drink.

In your journal write about one time in your life when you received blessing after a time of hardship or suffering.

Act of Commitment

Look for God and you will find God even as you seek.

Position: standing upright, feet slightly apart, hands by your sides.

- Lean forward at hips; put your hands above eyebrows as if to shade them from the sun. Keeping trunk parallel with floor scan the horizon from side to side in a wide sweep. Complete 8 slow swings from left to right. Stand up.
- Repeat scanning as above but this time bend trunk far enough to scan the ground. (If you are not fit, you may feel dizzy on standing up. Omit if you're not sure.)
- Standing upright, with hands still in scanning position, twist body to left and backwards, keeping feet still. Return to center (repeat 8 times).
- Repeat turning to right.
- Extend arms sideways. Swing body to left, then take weight on right leg as you swing your body right round to left to face in opposite direction. Swing back to start again (repeat 8 times).
- Repeat starting with a swing to right and taking weight on left foot as you turn.

(Rest if there's time to spare.)

Centering down

(start meditative music before centering)

Position: lying flat on your back.

Look up at the ceiling and allow your imagination to carry you through the roof towards the sky above.

Follow your eyes with your mind so that you are 'floating' upwards.

Enjoy that sensation and stay at peace with yourself.

Prayer for a meeting

In the stillness become aware of God's abiding presence. *'O Lord you have searched me and you know me. You know when I sit and when I rise;'* (Ps 139: 1-2.)

Meditation

Equipment: a mirror which can stand or be propped up; a candle and some matches.

Light your candle and put in front of mirror.

On our journey we are sustained by hope, hope that is fed by moments of vision when we are aware of God's glory, even though we cannot see it. Between those moments we travel by hope:

'And we rejoice in the hope of the glory of God. Not only so, but we also rejoice in our sufferings, because we know that suffering produces perseverance; perseverance, character; and character, hope. And hope does not disappoint us, because God has poured out his love into our hearts by the Holy Spirit whom he has given us.' (Rom 5: 2b-5.)

Think back over the past two months.

How has perseverance helped your character? How has hope 'not disappointed' you?

Action for the day: your candle represents Christ, the light of the world. Warm your hands by cupping them round it. Look at the reflection in the mirror before blowing out the candle and keeping it alight in yourself.

Later reflection

Kneel and center down. Light your candle again.

Warm your hands. Thank God for the moments of vision you have experienced and for the hope that is in you.

Pray that others may warm themselves by the flame of Christ's love.

In your journal describe any time in your life when hope has been born out of suffering.

If you cannot think along these lines, describe an occasion when hope was fulfilled for you.

Act of Commitment

Walk on now in the strength of the Spirit who directs your going and your coming.

Position: lying flat on your back on the floor, hands under your head, elbows bent.

- Raise left leg slowly, keeping toes pointed. Bring to right angle with floor to count of 4. Flex foot to stretch leg muscles tight. Hold to count of 4. Lower leg to same count (repeat 4 times).
- Repeat with right leg.
- Pull abdominal muscles in; repeat with both legs. (If you're not yet fit, this will be difficult – try it with hands by your sides.)
- Repeat but when your legs are at right angle to floor, open them widely in a V. Do this slowly to count of 4, but then snap shut. (If you can't manage this yet, try it with hands by your sides, pressing down on floor.)
- Put hands on hips. Turn feet in to press against each other, bending knees into a 'frog' position as you do so. Sit up, pushing off floor with arms if you have to. Lie down again (repeat 4 times).

Centering down

Position: sitting in a comfortable cross-legged position, on floor or cushion.

Focus your attention on your breathing. As you breathe out whisper to yourself '*Holy Spirit*', and say '*Come to me*' as you breathe in.

Continue until you feel at peace with yourself and your environment.

Prayer for a meeting

When you are still, ask God for help today: *Breathe on me breath of God. Fill me with life anew.*

editation

quipment: your notebook,
n or pencil; a ruler.

is is a thinking meditation
roughout, so first close
ur eyes for a moment and
k the Holy Spirit to guide
u.

ad aloud:

But the fruit of the Spirit
s love, joy, peace,
patience, kindness,
goodness, faithfulness,
gentleness and self-
control. Against such
things there is no law.
Those who belong to
Christ Jesus have
crucified the sinful nature
with its passions and
desires. Since we live by
he Spirit, let us keep in
step with the Spirit. Let us
not become conceited,
provoking and envying
one another.' (Gal 5:
22-26.)

your notebook list the
it: love for, joy about;
ace towards; patience
h; kindness towards; self-
ntrol about. Rule out two
lumns. In one write names
loveable objects, people
qualities you want to
hance (eg Love for – my
other, faithfulness about –
ayer.) In the other list the
itudes you need to
ange in yourself towards
emies or habits you
slike (eg love for my father
om I hate, faithfulness
out bible reading, which I
like.)

tion for the day: choose
e enemy and one friend
have named. Pray, with
m in mind, for all three of
u.

Later reflection

Curl up in your easy chair with your
notebook and pen. Relax and center
down.

Recall the names of the two people you
prayed for and with earlier in the day.
Pray for them again, using the Lord's
prayer with them in mind separately.

In your journal select two qualities
listed as 'fruit of the Spirit' and reflect
on their value in your own life.

Act of Commitment

As you touch your body with reverence, touch also the 'self' who is made in God's own image, and give glory to God who gave you your life.

Position: sitting cross-legged on floor or cushion, straight backed, with hands on knees, palms downwards.

- Lift both hands and gently and lovingly caress your head, face and neck. Then replace hands on knees (repeat 4 times, trying to learn more about yourself each time).
- Bend right down and kiss the hand on your left knee. Sit up again slowly (repeat 4 times).
- Repeat bending to kiss right hand.
- Uncross your legs. Spread them out in an extended V in front of you. Pull your body tall, then lean forward towards the left, reach out with hands and pointed fingers to touch left leg and try to kiss your left knee. Sit up (repeat 4 times).
- Repeat reaching for right leg and kissing right knee.
- Try to kiss the floor between your legs. You may not be able to do this yet if your hips are not as flexible as they should be by now! Keep trying.

Centering down

Position: sitting comfortably on floor or cushion.

Cover your face with the fingers and palms of both hands. Enjoy the warmth of your own breath.

Let your mind become very still and your heart ready to respond to Jesus, your friend and brother.

Prayer for a meeting

God is nearer to you than the air you breathe. Christ dwells in you; that is why you can cherish your body without turning it into an idol. Thank God for it and turn both inwards and outwards to find Jesus, your brother.

Meditation

Equipment: your bible.

Close your eyes. Imagine yourself sitting by a fire on a cold night with the lights turned out and a friend by your side with whom you have just eaten.

What do you enjoy most about your friendships? How do you know when people have stopped being acquaintances and have become friends with you?

Read aloud:

'My command is this: Love each other as I have loved you. Greater love has no-one than this, that he lay down his life for his friends. You are my friends if you do what I command.' (John 15: 12-14.)

What do you think Jesus is asking you to do today? How will you 'lay down your life for your friend' today, not literally but figuratively?

Action for the day: open your bible. Read John 15: 15-17. Find another passage in the New Testament about friendship. If you're short of time, leave this till later in the day.

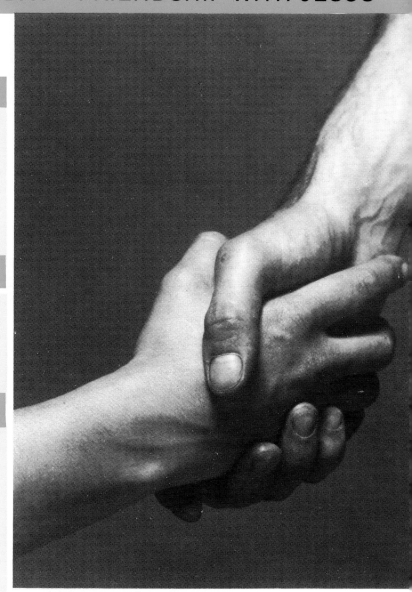

Later reflection

Sit in your comfortable chair with your bible to hand.

Did you meet any friends today?

Did you recognise your friend and brother, Jesus, today? How did you meet with him?

Find some of the interesting passages in the bible on friendship by looking in Proverbs: 27, 2 Cor: 2, Phil: 2.

In your journal write out the verses that speak to you most effectively today.

Act of Commitment

Fix your eyes on Jesus and run to win 'a crown that will last forever.'

Position: standing upright, ready to run. You can 'run on the spot', run indoors in small circles, or run outside. If you go out, take a 'timer' with you, so you can turn for home after two minutes.

- Start slowly, increase your pace to a jog or run which is comfortable; maintain that pace for the first three minutes.
- Once your body has settled into a rhythm, allow your mind to roam freely; notice the 'scenery', even if it is just the furniture in your own room, and let it speak to you. Think or pray without paying conscious attention to what your body is doing.
- After approximately three minutes, quicken your pace again to a sprint. Now bring your mind back again to bear on what your body is doing. Put all the effort you can into that last minute of running.
- Once you have, as it were 'passed the finishing tape', slow down as if you were coming to a standstill after a race.

Centering down

Position: kneeling upright and still with hands clasped at waist level.

Stay quite still and empty, waiting on God. You may be able to do this wordlessly now; if not, use the name of Jesus to steady you.

Be still until your 'timer' tells you it is time to pray.

Prayer for a meeting

Throw yourself into God's arms with the words, *'Thine for ever, God of love.'*

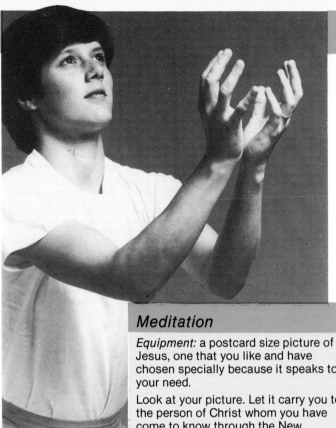

Meditation

Equipment: a postcard size picture of Jesus, one that you like and have chosen specially because it speaks to your need.

Look at your picture. Let it carry you to the person of Christ whom you have come to know through the New Testament.

What attracts you to Jesus? What qualities in you are like enough to Jesus to help you to grow closer to him? What 'gift' do you want to ask God for?

Read aloud:

'Let us fix our eyes on Jesus, the author and perfecter of our faith who for the joy set before him endured the cross, scorning its shame, and sat down at the right hand of the throne of God. Consider him who endured such opposition from sinful men, so that you will not grow weary and lose heart.' (Heb 12: 2-3.)

What things and which people in your life most help you to persevere in the Christian life, 'fixing your eyes on Jesus.'

Action for the day: put the picture of Jesus in your bible or prayer book. Add the price of that postcard to the money you have saved to give away. Double the total. That will be your offering for this journey. Give it to whom you will.

CCE REX TVVS VENIT TIBI MANSVETVS SEDES SV.P ASIÑA ZFILIV SVBIVGAL? CACHARI .IX.

ter reflection

d your easy chair and curl up in it.
ax and center down.

ank God for all that you have learnt
far on your Christian journey. Ask
d for the grace to persevere.

our journal begin to think about how
are going to continue your journey
en this particular one comes to an
d tomorrow.

SANNA FILIO DAVID BENEDICTVS QVI VENIT IN NOMINE DOMINI. MACTEI .XXI.

60 ÎMOLABO VOBIS VICTIMÃ SVP MONTEM VT OMEDATIS CARNES ZBIBATIS SANGVIÑE .ECECHI.XXXIX.

Act of Commitment

You have reached the end of this part of your journey. But there is no end to 'going on with Jesus'. Go on, then, and enjoy it.

Position: lying flat on your back, knees bent, feet together flat on the floor, hands by sides.

- Lift your buttocks off floor to balance on your heels and shoulders. Hold to count of 4. Lower body; rest for 4 counts (repeat 4 times).
- Roll your body back on to your shoulders. Lift buttocks and body into the air. (Put fisted hands under your buttocks if you need to.) Cycle vigorously for 8 revolutions. Then stop with legs vertically extended, toes pointed. Open your legs to form arch over head. Hold for count of 4. Lower yourself to floor (repeat 4 times).
- Change position to standing upright, feet together, hands on your hips. Keeping knees straight, head well tucked in, touch your toes. Rise to upright stance (repeat 8 times).
- Standing on left leg, high kick 4 times forwards with right leg, 4 times sideways, 4 times backwards.
- Repeat, standing on right leg and kicking with left.
- Do deep knees bend 8 times.

Centering down

Position: your own choice out of all you have tried over the past two months.

Wait on God knowing that 'your life is now hidden with Christ in God.' (Col. 3: 3.) *'Be still and know that I am God.'* (Ps 46:10.)

...yer for a meeting

...re is no end to 'going on with Jesus'.
... journey is but one of many in the
...pany of God's disciples and friends.
...nk God for its joys, lessons,
...ggles and growing points.

...ditation

...*pment:* some of the favourite things
...have used before. Arrange them as
...wish.

...w the objects you have gathered to
...k to you of your life as a Christian.

...nk God for all the times of testing
...have endured.

...d Paul's great words of confidence:

...or I am convinced that neither death
... life, neither angels nor demons,
...ther the present nor the future, nor
...y powers, neither height nor depth,
... anything else in all creation, will
... able to separate us from the love
...God that is in Christ Jesus our
...rd.' (Rom 8: 38-39.)

...nk God for those words and for your
...n.

... for those who do not have that
...sing.

...*on for the day:* keep some of your
...ipment' to remind you of this part of
... journey. Put them where they will
...se you.

Later reflection

Curl up in your comfortable chair. Relax
and center down.

Decide which parts of the course have
been most useful to you: which
exercises, methods of centering down,
prayers and meditations would you feel
able to carry on with?

In your journal note anything you feel
may help to set you free to undertake
the next part of your pilgrimage through
life.

Tomorrow you won't have any exercises
to do. It is important to have at least one
week's rest before deciding what to
do next.

'Stand firm then, with the belt of truth buckled round your waist, with the breastplate of righteousness in place, and with your feet fitted with the readiness that comes from the gospel of peace. In addition to all this, take up the shielf of faith, with which you can extinguish all the flaming arrows of the evil one. Take the helmet of salvation and the sword of the Spirit which is the word of God. And pray in the Spirit on all occasions with all kinds of prayers and requests. With this in mind, be alert and always keep on praying for all the saints.'

Eph 6: 14-18.

APPENDIX A

Bible quotations used

WEEK 1   CALL TO ADVENTURE

Sun	Matt	13:3b – 9	New beginnings
Mon	Matt	4:18 – 20	Travelling light
Tue	1 Ki	1:12 – 13	Food for sharing
Wed	Jer	1:6 – 8	Talents for service
Thu	Matt	4:21 – 22	Companionship on the way
Fri	Matt	16:24 – 26	Sacrificial love
Sat	Jer	18:3 – 6	Looking forward

WEEK 2   SETTING OUT

Sun	Josh	18:3 – 4	Making a survey
Mon	Luke	9 – 3 – 6	Taking only what you need
Tue	Luke	6:36 – 38	Giving and receiving
Wed	Isa	35:8 – 9	The way of holiness
Thu	Acts	8:30 – 31	Sharing a vision
Fri	Luke	19:3 – 6	Running towards God
Sat	Mark	10:21 – 22	Change of direction

WEEK 3   PROVISIONS FOR PILGRIMS

Sun	Matt	13:44 – 46	Seeking the kingdom
Mon	Ex	15:23 – 25a	Helping God to help us
Tue	Mark	6:37 – 38	Gifts from God
Wed	2 Tim	1:7 – 9	Endurance
Thu	Ruth	1:16 – 17a	Friendships
Fri	Luke	10:33 – 35	Detours of love
Sat	Num	9:18, 21b	Resting on the way

WEEK 4   GUIDELINES FOR LIVING

Sun	Matt	5:14 – 16	Lighted lamps for God
Mon	Matt	5:17, 19	Chained yet free
Tue	Matt	5:43 – 45	Love for enemies
Wed	Matt	6:3 – 4	Deeds of charity
Thu	Matt	6:9 – 13	United by God
Fri	Matt	7:3 – 5	Judgement
Sat	Matt	7:15 – 20	The fruits of love

WEEK 5   TRAVELLING COMPANIONS

Sun	Isa	6:1 – 3	In the company of angels
Mon	Job	37:10 – 13	Singing in the rain
Tue	Gen	1:29 – 30	Green fingers for God
Wed	Ex	23:12	Travels with a donkey
Thu	Ps	150:1, 3 – 6	The friendly arts
Fri	Matt	25:37 – 40	Christ in each other
Sat	Eccl	3:1 – 4	Seasons and rhythms

WEEK 6   MANNA IN THE DESERT

Sun	Mark	1:12 – 13	Desert journey
Mon	John	1:29 – 30	Lightening the load
Tue	John	6:30 – 32	God's gifts in the desert
Wed	1 Cor	10:12 – 13	Learning to survive
Thu	1 Pet	4:12 – 14	The fellowship of suffering
Fri	Rom	15:1 – 2	Rides for stragglers
Sat	Rom	8:23 – 25	Renewal of hope

WEEK 7   LEAPS AND LANDINGS

Sun	2 Ki	2:13 – 14	Old mantles on new shoulders
Mon	2 Ki	5:13 – 14	Little leaps, big landings
Tue	2 Ki	6:21 – 22	Unexpected mercies
Wed	Luke	5:37 – 38	New wine in new wineskins
Thu	Acts	10:30 – 33	Landing in neighbours' patches
Fri	Ex	4:11 – 14a, 15	Letting go
Sat	Mark	5:27 – 29	Happy landings

WEEK 8   NEW HORIZONS

Sun	2 Cor	5:17 – 20a	New creatures in Christ
Mon	John	14:2b – 4	Travelling with Jesus
Tue	Rom	5:2b – 5	Vision of glory
Wed	Gl	5:22 – 26	Walking by the spirit
Thu	John	15:12 – 14	Friendship with Jesus
Fri	Heb	12:2 – 3	Running with endurance
Sat	Rom	8:38 – 39	Going on with Jesus

APPENDIX B

Structure of each day's programme

PHASE A

Time: fifteen minutes sometime in the day, preferably in the morning

Activity
- 'Warm up' exercises
- Centering down to stillness
- Prayer for a meeting
- Meditation on a biblical theme
- Resolution and action for the day

PHASE B

Time: noon, or some other fixed point in the day

Activity
- The daily recitation of the Lord's prayer

PHASE C

Time: fifteen extra minutes at a separate time of day

Activity
- Relaxation
- Reflection
- Keeping a spiritual journal

Phase A needs to be a regular daily event in your life.

Phase B and Phase C are 'extras' for those who have the time and inclination to spend some energy complementing and expanding Phase A insights.

APPENDIX C

Equipment for meditations

WEEK 1   CALL TO ADVENTURE

Sun   A single seed which could be planted
Mon   3 stones, small enough to handle
Tue   Flour & salt in jar; small jug of oil; water; bowl; plate
Wed   Full jug of water; empty glass
Thu   Notebook; pen or pencil
Fri   3 coins of equal value; matching sum of money; home-made cross
Sat   Plasticine, or other modelling material

WEEK 2   SETTING OUT

Sun   Pair of socks and shoes
Mon   One small stone
Tue   A flower; or a picture of one
Wed   Working notebook; pen or pencil
Thu   Bible: working notebook; pen or pencil
Fri   Notebook; smallest coin in your pocket or purse
Sat   Notebook; pen or pencil

WEEK 3   PROVISIONS FOR PILGRIMS

Sun   Jar of rice containing different seed; small bowl
Mon   Cup of tea made with tea leaves
Tue   2 identically wrapped packets: (1) raisins (2) nuts
Wed   Box of matches; candle; needle & thread
Thu   Pair of shoes; bible
Fri   Jug of oil; small bowl; towel to wipe hands
Sat   Small pillow; blanket; an alarm clock

WEEK 4   GUIDELINES FOR LIVING

Sun   2 candles; matches; bible
Mon   A long piece of string; bible
Tue   Working notebook; pen or pencil
Wed   2 small empty bowls; 2 coins of equal value
Thu   7 stones; kitchen foil; a plastic bag
Fri   Bowl of water; towel; sum of money equal to cost of towel
Sat   A twig from bush or tree; or picture of one

WEEK 5   TRAVELLING COMPANIONS

Sun   Bible; any picture of an angel
Mon   Water in a bowl; candle and matches
Tue   Piece of ripe fruit; edible raw vegetable; flowers or leaves in vase
Wed   Picture of domesticated farm animal (eg. cow or horse)
Thu   Any beautiful picture or postcard; short poem or prose piece
Fri   Notebook; pen or pencil; coin of moderate value
Sat   Notebook; pen or pencil

WEEK 6   MANNA IN THE DESERT

Sun   Bible; notebook; pen or pencil
Mon   Heavy weight (eg. books or sack of potatoes); paper; matches
Tue   Piece of bread; glass of water; bible
Wed   Notebook; pen or pencil; humility
Thu   Cross made of twigs or cardboard; notebook; pen or pencil
Fri   A mirror; some money
Sat   Handful of sand, or 'sand' (salt) in bowl; notebook; pen or pencil

WEEK 7   LEAPS AND LANDINGS

Sun   A long necklace; chain or scarf
Mon   Bible
Tue   Glass of water and empty jug
Wed   2 polythene bags; half glass of water; bowl; bible
Thu   Candle; icon or holy picture; small statue; matches; bible
Fri   Ball; price of that ball in money
Sat   Yourself as you are today; notebook; pen or pencil

WEEK 8   NEW HORIZONS

Sun   Plasticine or other modelling material
Mon   Water in medium sized bowl
Tue   Mirror; candle; matches
Wed   Notebook; pen or pencil; ruler
Thu   Bible
Fri   Postcard-sized picture of Jesus; money equal to its price
Sat   Some of your favourite equipment, used before

APPENDIX D

Selected Bibliography

GENERAL

1   Gordon Rattray Taylor, *The Natural History of the Mind* Secker & Warburg, 1979.
2   Frithof Capra, *The Tao of Physics* Wildwood House, 1979.
3   Gary Zukov, *The Dancing Wu Li Masters* Rider/Hutchinson, 1979.
4   Alvin Toffler, *Future Shock* Bodley Head, 1970.
5   U. Kroll, *A Signpost for the World* Darton, Longman & Todd, 1974.

BOOKS ON HEALING

1   Evelyn Frost, *Christian Healing* Mowbray, 1940/1949.
2   F. McNutt, *Healing* Ave Maria Press, 1974.
3   J.A. Sanford, *Healing and Wholeness* Paulist Press/A. James Ltd, 1982.
4   J.A. Sanford, *Ministry Burnout* Paulist Press, 1978.
5   D. & M. Linn, *Healing Life's Hurts* Paulist Press, 1978.
6   D. & M. & M.J. Linn, *Healing the Dying* Paulist Press, 1979.
7   L. Chaitow, *Relaxations and Meditation Techniques* Thorson's Publishers, 1983.
8   B. Kidman, *A Gentle Way with Cancer* Century Publishing, 1983.

BOOKS ON SPIRITUALITY IN PRACTICE

1   T. Kelly, *A Testament of Devotion* Quaker Home Service, 1979.
2   R. Foster, *Celebration of Discipline* Hodder & Stoughton, 1980.
3   R. Foster, *The Freedom of Simplicity* Harper & Row/Triangle/S.P.C.K., 1981.
4   E.H. Patery, *Christian Life Style* Mowbray, 1976.
5   D. Nicholson, *Holiness* Darton, Longmann & Todd, 1981.
6   C de Hueck Doherty, *Poutinia* Collins/Fontana, 1977.
7   W. Johnston, *The Inner Eye of Love* Collins/Fount, 1978.
8   Tr. C. Wolters, *The Cloud of Unknowing* Penguin, 1961.
9   R. Llwelwyn, *Without Pity, Without Blame* Darton, Longmann & Todd, 1984.
10 M. Kelsey, *Adventure Inward: Christian Growth through Journal Writing* Minneapolis, 1980.
11 H. Nouwen, *The Genesee Diary* Doubleday, N.Y., 1981.